How They Started

ABER

D0264365

How
They
Started

How 30 good ideas
became great businesses

David Lester

Lester, David

How they started : how
30 good ideas became

Y658.
11

1942919

This edition first published in Great Britain in 2007 by
Crimson Publishing
Westminster House
Kew Road
Richmond
Surrey
TW9 2ND

© David Lester 2007
Reprinted 2008

The right of David Lester to be identified as the author of this work has been asserted
by him in accordance with the Copyright, Designs and Patents Act, 1988.

All rights reserved. No part of this publication may be reproduced, transmitted in any
form or by any means, or stored in a retrieval system without either the prior written
permission of the publisher, or in the case of reprographic reproduction a licence
issued in accordance with the terms and licences issued by the CLA Ltd.

A catalogue record for this book is available from the British library.

ISBN 978 1 85458 400 7

Printed in Great Britain by Ashford Colour Press Ltd., Gosport, Hampshire

Contents

Foreword

When we started Innocent we discovered just what an emotional rollercoaster starting a business is. The three of us quit good jobs to pursue an idea that we believed could go somewhere. Eventually it did, but it took a lot of time, determination and patience. It's not an easy journey.

Like a lot of people just starting out, we hadn't read much about how other people had set up their own businesses. We would have found this book a huge help – if only to strengthen our resolve that we weren't completely mad to carry on!

Above all what I love about this book is the passion and commitment from so many people who've taken an idea and overcome all kinds of obstacles to build a thriving business. Each story is different, some very personal, some surprising, but all are encouraging.

If you go on to start your own business after reading this, I wish you the best of luck with it. And remember, enjoy it, and keep the main thing the main thing.

Richard Reed

innocent
little tasty drinks

Acknowledgements

I would especially like to thank the people whose businesses we have written about in this book. Each of them has given generously both detailed information about sometimes distant memories, and their time, which as we all know is our most precious commodity these days, and they have done so for no return other than the knowledge that they might help others – thank you.

As Editor, I would like to thank the authors, who have written most of the profiles in this book. They are: Beth Law, Lianne Slavin, Matt Thomas, Jon Card, Stephanie Welstead, Kate Dunn, and Jeff Meyer; and also Ian Wallis, Sara Rizk and Oliver Milman for their assistance with interviews.

I would particularly like to thank the Crimson Publishing team who have made this book happen, namely Holly Bennion, Mark Edwards, Lucy Smith, John O'Toole, Beth Law, Lianne Slavin, Ella Gascoigne and Carol Farley, our PR consultant. As Crimson's first business book, publishing it has taken more from us than we expect in future.

And lastly, I would like to thank my two sons, Oliver and Jonny, who have put up, mainly happily, with my working more than expected to complete this; and Sue, my wife, who has willingly taken up the slack with childcare and running our lives that my extra working hours have left.

Introduction

Almost all of us have at some time or other come away from an experience and thought that it must be possible to deliver a better service or product. Most of us mutter and grumble a bit, then move on. A smaller number of us continue to develop the idea gently, before gradually moving on from it. What makes the people described in this book different is that they took an idea just like the ones we have had, then they developed it, and then they launched a business based on it which went on to be highly successful.

Which brings me to why we decided to write this book. This book is for all of you who have had those ideas, whether you have developed them at this stage or not. My hope is that the book will both inform and inspire you. Some of you, I hope, will go on to start your own businesses after reading these uplifting tales, and I certainly hope that you will be better prepared for what will happen. But I also hope that some of you will decide, after reading this, that starting your own business is perhaps not for you after all. That should not get in the way of your enjoyment of this, or of your dreaming; perhaps it will be that you simply haven't found the right idea yet.

I cannot imagine anyone reading this book and not then having several ideas for new businesses within a few weeks. And if so, what a wonderful result, regardless of whether those ideas turn into businesses or not; positive dreams about our futures play a wonderful role in our wellbeing. And I hope that you feel better able to consider which of your ideas might really be worth pursuing.

Some people believe that successful small-business people are born, not made; that you either have it, or you don't. Some of the entrepreneurs profiled in this book express opinions about this which we have included. We can't answer that for you – we have not set out to make this book a definitive test of whether you could succeed running your own business; rather, we have set out to show some of the highs and some of the lows along the way, showing a wide variety of different obstacles that real startup businesses have encountered, as a way of showing the sort of issues you might well face in your own startup.

One of the wonderful things to jump out of this book is just how disparate the founders are. This is not entirely coincidental, but it does nonetheless show that you don't need a very particular background to be able to make your own business succeed.

Please remember, too, that we have only covered here businesses that have thrived. We set out to do this, to show that it is very possible to create a substantial business from literally just an idea. But it is all too easy to get carried away by the fact that all the businesses we have written about in this book have overcome their problems. Of course they have – but literally hundreds of thousands of businesses have been started which ran into similar problems which were not overcome, and as a result those businesses are no longer around. We have probably never heard of most of them, but that doesn't make the pain suffered by their founders any less.

I have started several businesses myself, which have succeeded, and been involved in or very close to more than a dozen other startups, not all of which have made it. I have also seen enough results from venture capitalists who invest in startups to know that the chances of new businesses succeeding and thriving are very slim. I know from my own experience that it is both enormously satisfying to create a successful business from scratch, and also extremely hard. To try to get people to buy from your new business in sufficient quantity to make it viable is a real challenge – far harder than to grow something which already exists.

When I first came up with all my new business ideas, many people asked me why, if it was such a good idea, nobody else had done it. It is a really important question, and before you start your own new venture, I suggest that you try to come up with some good answers; try to satisfy yourself, deep down, that you are comfortable that the idea really is good even though no one has done it before. And sleep on it, as my father used to tell me; it is amazing how often you can spot a glaring error in a plan the day after it looked unbeatable!

Interestingly, several people have asked me during the writing of this book whether it has been done before. And indeed, there are one or two books out there which sound as though they might cover the same ground. But they don't. Our entire focus is on how people take an idea and turn it into a business, and this is the first book to go into anything like this detail about that, which also means we have had to put in roughly twice as much information to every business we cover. I think this is significant – after all, it is that first phase which is the hardest. And of course, blowing my own trumpet for a moment, this is definitely the only book of its kind to be edited by someone who has started several businesses; I hope you will yield the benefit of that in some of the details included.

Let me leave you with one final thought. When we produce our next edition of this book, do you think will we want your new business to be covered?

I hope you enjoy the book.

David Lester
Founder, Startups.co.uk and
Managing Director, Crimson Publishing

How did we select the companies for this book?

We set out to find a wide variety of businesses, focussing on the sort of businesses most people think about starting, in other words avoiding less practical ideas such as oil refining or airliner manufacturing! From there, we applied three strict criteria:

- Firstly, and most importantly, every company we cover was started by one or more individuals who had an idea. None of them had any unfair or unusual advantage, such as a parent who owned a major supplier.

- Secondly, every business we cover here is successful.

- Thirdly, they are all also 'a household name'.

This is important for two reasons; firstly, because you, the reader, are much more likely to know many of the businesses we profile here, which should mean that their journey from idea to viable business takes on much more practical meaning for you – you should understand what each step and decision means for the business. And secondly, because many of you are simply fascinated by how some of these well-known names got started.

To be fair, we have included some businesses that are well-known in their sector, but which are not strictly speaking 'household names'. Jigsaw Research, MeetingZone, One Small Step, Extreme Group, and arguably The Cinnamon Club, all fall into this category. We selected them because they meet our two fundamental criteria, and because we wanted to add two more – diversity of company, and stage of business. We wanted to show that it is still possible today for normal people to take a great idea and turn it into a viable, thriving business.

We expect all our less well-known businesses to go on to be highly successful and significant within their markets. We expect most of them will also one day become household names.

Above all, we wanted to show that businesses started by one or a small group of people from a good idea can go on to become very substantial indeed.

What can we learn from these businesses as a group?

The X Factor

It is impossible not to try to compare the different stories in a book such as this, to see if there is some apparent natural formula for success. Luckily for us all, there really is no single 'one type of person fits all' answer. Men and women of different ages, from a variety of racial, educational and family backgrounds, have taken an idea and turned it into a wonderful business. Even experience levels of a particular sector seem to matter remarkably little with this group of ultra successful people (though this is perhaps more important in some sectors than others).

But all the people in this book shared a number of ways of behaving which I think is crucial to their success. It's not what they were or had to start with that made them a success, but how they went about it. No single X factor, then – but a group of X factors.

Minimal personal reward initially

Almost all the founders we profiled spent many months or even years taking out very little personally from the businesses they were starting. In some cases the businesses simply could not provide any more income, in others the founders wanted to leave the cash in the business to help give it a chance to put down some roots and grow. A significant minority of the founders started the business as a part-time activity while they carried on with their day jobs to fund their living expenses, focusing full-time on their own business when it had shown enough potential to make them take that leap.

Do what it says on the tin

All the new businesses in this book started out with a real focus on one idea. That is quite normal for startups – and is a huge advantage. Doing almost anything for the first time is more special, more exciting than doing it the seventy-fifth time. For many people setting up their own business, there is a wonderful combination of being passionate and driven to achieve something, at the same time as a sense of wonder and amazement when the business actually works. This helps all the young businesses we feature here stay committed to their original vision, which sets them apart from their competition.

Keep it simple

Very often established companies feel a need to add new twists or features for the sake of it; frequently this drive for change can take over, with customers' needs forgotten or subconsciously put to one side. The businesses in this book all succeeded by staying close to their customer, keeping their business very simple (almost none of them added potentially distracting other divisions); focus seems to matter massively.

Work harder than you might think possible

Sad but true. Eighteen hour days are pretty common when talking to these entrepreneurs. None of the founders started out as workaholics – they all began as normal people just like you. Yet all of them were sufficiently committed that when work needed to be done, they did it, even if it took them past the standard 37.5 hours a week. And I do think this is significant; all new businesses need to start momentum in their sector; it takes substantial effort to start anything moving, far less effort when it's started – as true for a business as for a car. Perween Warsi's story particularly stands out here amongst many who encountered this.

Keep trying and believing

About half the businesses in this book had early sales substantially below what they needed to be viable. Some of them picked up very rapidly indeed, made far more possible by the internet, but most product businesses had to cope with a longer wait than they had planned before the money started coming in. All too often newspapers report on 'overnight millionaires' when a founder floats or sells their company; there is almost never anything 'overnight' about it – starting a successful business takes a long time. Even Innocent, one of the most successful startups of the last decade, struggled initially. Every business we cover has had to overcome significant issues to keep trading, let alone succeed; along their way, each founder faced doubt, anxiety, stress and pressure level way beyond what most employees face; their ability to cope with this, almost always deeply rooted in strong self belief, was an important factor in why they succeeded where so many businesses haven't.

Who needs money?

All businesses need some money to start with. About a quarter of the founders raised funds from business angels to get started. Another quarter raised venture capital later on, to grow their business faster than would have been possible otherwise. And the often criticised banks have put more money up, and with less security, than many of us might have predicted. Which means that roughly half the businesses managed to start without significant cash from outside investors – very encouraging news for many, I'm sure. The businesses which did not need serious outside investment initially tended to be either service businesses, such as Stopgap, or where the founders were established in their field already, such as Codemasters.

Ambition

Not one of the founders we spoke to set out to become significantly wealthy. Their reasons for starting varied from needing to earn a living after redundancy to wanting a certain quality of product or service which didn't previously exist, or even simply wanting to see if they could succeed within an exciting, fast growing market. This is quite different to many people's expectations, but very typical of entrepreneurs I meet; very occasionally I come across someone who set out to become rich, but only very rarely. I think the passion and commitment needed to become as successful as the businesses in this book now are, have to be the primary driving forces within the founders, rather than to get rich. To work the hours, take the risks, make the personal life sacrifices all the founders here have done, takes very, very strong motivation; very few people who say they want to build a business in order to get rich have anything like that degree of motivation.

So what?

It seems clear that to succeed with their own business, these founders didn't need money or education or family connections. They all had a clear idea for a product or service which some part of the world needed and couldn't get before they started. And they needed literally extra-ordinary levels of passion, energy, self belief and stamina, the ability and desire to focus, and a good measure of judgement.

CHOCOLATE PUDS

Gü Chocolate Puds

The Sweet Taste of Success

Company:	**Gü Chocolate Puds**
Founder:	**James Averdieck**
Age at start:	**37**
Background:	**Worked for St Ivel for nine years in sales and marketing**
Start year:	**2003**
Business:	**Desserts and puddings**

J ames Averdieck, founder of Gü Chocolate Puds, the high quality desserts and puddings company, has cooked up a series of products that have found their way remarkably rapidly into over 3,000 supermarkets in the UK, as well many other food retailers. James spotted a gap in the market: there was a serious lack of high quality desserts that could be bought and consumed at home. Since launching in 2003, Gü Chocolate Puds has grown into a business which generated revenues of £7.5 million in 2005 and projects to double that amount in 2006.

Entrepreneurial Ambition

James had always wanted to be an entrepreneur, and other members of his family, his brothers, father, grandfather, had run their own businesses. 'It's in the blood' he says. He had run other ventures while he was at university and feels that it was only a matter of time before he did so again. His family have been a constant source of advice and his father drummed into him the belief that the key to a successful business was 'having the right product'. James says that the view might be obvious, but it is a crucial part of a business that many people fail to get right.

James noticed that many of the fine desserts found in the patisseries of France and Belgium were often not available in the UK. There were also very few brands associated with high quality desserts, and he thought the British public could do with one. It was an industry that he knew well as he was a member of the board at St Ivel, the desserts company and had previous experience at Safeway. He thought that British tastes were more sophisticated than the range on offer in most supermarkets suggested, and that, when it came down to it, 'Brits love a decent pudding'. He also believed that many people who hosted dinner parties were accustomed to eating at good restaurants, but perhaps lacked the skills or time to make their own pudding. Therefore, he mused, the chance to buy a ready-made but still top quality dessert would be popular with many people.

James decided to create a 'premium brand' that captured the essence of good chocolate and was the sort of food that you could buy in, for instance, a good patisserie in Paris.

James saw himself as more of a 'sales and marketing guy' so he knew he needed someone who could provide the food and manufacturing side of the business. However, while he was still working for St Ivel, he had come to know a company called Rensow Patisserie, at a trade show in Spain in 2000. They were well established in the airline food industry and were looking to open up new lines of business.

In Rensow, he saw a business that could manufacture good quality food in an efficient way. James knew the retail market and was confident he could do the selling, so the partners felt that they 'covered all the bases'.

Gü's ramekin packs.

James mused over his idea for some time until in January 2003 the joint venture was put together with an initial investment of circa £100,000. The company, which was later to become known as Gü, began creating its products based partly on the foods that James had sampled on the continent.

The first product they designed was a chocolate pudding presented in a glass ramekin. James felt that the quality of the food and its presentation meant that it had a restaurant quality, it could also be customised by the consumer and, perhaps, even passed off as their own creation.

'Gü is a really good solution to the question "what am I going to serve my guests for pudding?"' James asserts. 'It has a home-made quality but also it has a convenience as well.'

Creating the Brand

Although James believed he had both a great product and that there was a gap in the market, he knew that in order to establish the business in the market he would also require a great brand. Despite a background in sales and marketing himself, he felt his business needed something special, so he hired a branding company, Big Fish, who had experience in conceiving and designing premium brands, to design the packaging logos for his business and, perhaps most importantly come up with the name. He was in a good position to approach such a company as he knew the market that he was selling to and so he could outline his typical buyer to them. He took his products with him so the company could actually experience the product themselves. Big Fish were impressed with James' product and wanted to work with him.

This was a considerable risk on Gü's part as he had to outlay a significant amount of money, and he was also putting the future of his company into someone else's hands. However, Big Fish had an impressive client list and experience of working with premium brands. The company also show considerable passion for James' business.

The director of Big Fish, Perry Haydn Taylor, loved James' product and conceived of the Gü brand himself. The brand was the only idea that he came up with but he decided to sell it to James in a somewhat unorthodox manner. Perry told James that the Gü brand would be perfect, however he also fabricated that it already belonged to a European company.

'They showed it to me and I thought "what a brilliant name, but ... they've beaten us to it!" – I was totally hooked,' James remembers.

Certain that the brand was right Taylor revealed the truth and James took the name as his own. However, he wanted to test the brand out. So he took some of the early product boxes and cheekily slipped them on to the shelf of his local supermarket. He then stood back and watched the shoppers take them off the shelf – further proof that he had a winner.

'A brand encapsulates the essence of what you are selling: when I was shown Gü for the first time I just knew "that's us".'

James says, 'a brand encapsulates the essence of what you are selling: when I was shown Gü for the first time I just knew "that's us".'

Today, James refers to the Gü brand as his 'number one advertisement' and clearly has no regrets of his decision to get an expert in to do the branding, and Big Fish still designs the packaging for their products to this day.

'I think you have to seduce your customers twice: once with the packaging and then again with the product itself. If you do that you will have loyal customers,' James says.

Cracking the Supermarkets

In order to sell Gü in the massive quantities that he wanted, James knew that he had to get his products into the supermarkets. His previous experience in the market was, of course, a major benefit to him, but selling a new product to supermarkets from an unknown new company is a very tough nut to crack.

He knew from his experience at St Ivel that even if they liked the product, the supermarkets would need satisfying about lots of issues such as food safety, factory

Gü kings of choc'n roll: Elvis party puds.   *Hot chocolate soufflés.*

hygiene and ability to fulfil demand. However, as his business partner was already an established food manufacturer many of the tough questions could be confidently answered. But nevertheless he was no longer working for St Ivel and was now the head of a new company with no prior history.

'Supermarket buyers aren't there to do your business plan for you. They are incredibly busy people and are approached constantly with new ideas. To stand out from the rest of the pack you need to offer real innovation.'

'I feel also that it is really important that you actually get to meet the buyers so that they can see the passion that has gone into the product' James suggests. 'In my case it was a question of calling the right people and immediately establishing credentials to get that initial meeting.'

'Supermarket buyers aren't there to do your business plan for you... You have to be prepared to answer their questions and meet their demands.'

Gü launched with Waitrose and Sainsbury's in June 2003. Others followed and a year later Gü was supplying puddings the length and breadth of the country. However, despite Gü's success, James is determined to avoid becoming complacent. The battle for shelf space is continuous and there are always other products that are waiting, if yours do not work.

There is also the constant pressure of making and supplying their stores seven days a week. Gü employed a distribution company to take on some of the strain but it was the responsibility of James to ensure that the orders were fulfilled.

'Logistics in the UK are the most sophisticated in the world, and the most demanding,' he says. 'It is a case of monitoring what's going on and trying to piggy-back on other companies' deliveries by buying a bit of space in their trucks.'

WHERE ARE THEY NOW?

Since it began trading Gü has extended its product lines and now has a range of puddings, soufflés and ice cream. The company brand has become enormously successful and James Averdieck now buys other products that he likes and uses the Gü brand to sell them. The company employs more than 40 staff and James says that his company is expected to make revenues of £11.5 million in 2006.

Hotel du Vin & Bistro

WINCHESTER

Hotel Du Vin

Room For Improvement

Company:	Hotel Du Vin
Founders:	Robin Hutson and Gerard Basset
Age at start:	Both 37
Background:	Robin was Managing Director at top hotel Chewton Glen with 20 years of experience and Gerard was Head Sommelier for six years, and trained as a chef in France
Start year:	1994
Business:	Hotel and Bistro

(Courtesy of Tom Stockill Photography)

Hotel du Vin was an immediate success. By filling a gaping hole in the hospitality market for an affordable but stylish establishment outside London, Hotel du Vin easily and quickly seized custom from the less appealing, similar priced hotels it left in its wake. With experienced management and a superb sommelier, Hotel du Vin replaced dim rooms decked in chintzy upholstery with bright, airy ones featuring handsprung mattresses, fine Egyptian linen, deep baths and power showers which all seemed to draw in, and retain, customers.

Begun in 1994 in the small yet bustling town of Winchester only a stones throw outside of London, the 'micro-chain' now comprises nine hotels and is still expanding. It was not the intention to become a chain at first; the primary concern was to make one small provincial hotel a success, and with it, create a fresh new style of accommodation.

The idea of Hotel du Vin was conceived while its founders worked together at the luxury Hampshire hotel Chewton Glen. Robin Hutson had been the Managing Director there for eight years and at 38, felt ready to start a business of his own. He easily persuaded Gerard Basset, who had been Head Sommelier at the hotel for six years, to join him and bring his wine expertise to the venture.

'You were more likely to have a bad experience in a provincial hotel than a good one. I thought it really didn't have to be that bad.'

Robin and Gerard saw a gap in the market for a reasonably priced hotel outside of London that did not compromise on service or quality. They thought they could enhance this with an excellent wine list, a bistro restaurant, and a relaxed, homely atmosphere, all things which were missing from most regional hotels at the time. Before they started, 'you were more likely to have a bad experience in a provincial hotel than a good one' says Gerard. Hotel du Vin changed all that.

The partners remained at Chewton Glen while they put together the plan for their own hotel. Meeting in secret, sharing ideas in Robin's office and having to contact investors privately proved a challenging environment in which to form a business plan. Juggling a full-time job with the demands of beginning a business was far from ideal, but was unavoidable as both needed the income from their jobs before they risked embarking on their own venture.

The exterior of the first hotel in Winchester.

In a perfect world, being able to take your time creating and executing a business plan is of course preferable when starting a business. But Robin suggests that this problem may have made them even more determined to succeed. 'It would have been very easy to fail before we got started just because it was very hard raising the money when we only had a half-arsed business plan and no real track record as operators.'

Once they had decided that their idea for a new type of hotel was worth pursuing, Robin and Gerard needed to raise money – setting up a new hotel needs a great deal of capital. The first step was to solidify their business plan to show how much money they would need, and how much they might make if the business worked. They took this plan to a bank and lots of potential investors.

It took around six months and plenty of twists and turns to raise the money. The partners quickly learnt that there was a huge gulf between investors promising to invest and actually writing the cheque. Whilst they experienced disappointment along the way, they were delighted in the end as unexpected investors came up with the goods. Robin puts this success down to their well thought out plan and their

'There is a huge difference between people saying they're going to put money into something and actually writing the cheque.'

Gerard and Robin during the planning process. (Courtesy of Tom Stockill Photography)

passion for the project. He also comments that they 'sold it on the basis of a lifestyle investment backed by freehold property and experienced management'. Robin recalls that most investors they approached were enthusiastic. He puts this down to the strength of the business idea – others also recognised the gap in the market and wanted to capitalise on the anticipated trend for an out-of-town, boutique hotel. They eventually found 14 private investors prepared to contribute £500,000 and received a £750,000 bank loan from the Royal Bank of Scotland.

Even with this much funding in their kitty they had no money to spare, so the first hotel was completed on a 'shoestring' budget. By being very careful how they spent the money they managed not to cut corners and still produced quality without blowing their budget. For example, unlike many upper-end hotels, Hotel du Vin does not clean your shoes if you leave them outside your room, or leave chocolates on your pillow. This all bumps up the overall price of a room and is an unnecessary extravagance. Instead, Hotel du Vin focuses on comfortable beds, a nice shower, good wine and good food. Thus, its income is fairly evenly distributed between accommodation costs and food and drink, and produces quality without the frills.

Confidence in Difference

The partners had total confidence in their idea. Robin anticipated a 'wave of change' about to happen in the hospitality industry and placed Hotel du Vin at the forefront. Their self-belief also lay in the amount of experience the partners were bringing to a relatively small project. Naturally, the founders experienced some pre-opening nerves but their worries were not realised.

'People say the first few months are your honeymoon period, after which you will probably hit bad patches. It didn't happen.'

From the first day, Hotel du Vin was a success. Robin worked hard to ensure the opening was well documented in the media but did not spend a fortune on a marketing campaign – they did not have the money for one. Instead, he called journalist contacts of his and invited them to visit. This worked wonders at minimal cost and Hotel du Vin was applauded for its personal approach and affordable excellence. One month after they had opened, Jonathan Meades, the influential food critic for *The Times*, wrote a very complimentary article that really boosted interest in the hotel. Meades gave the hotel a rating of 6/10 (he could often give as little as two or three), which Gerard comments was 'perfect for us'. It was complimentary enough to raise awareness and interest, but not so much as to raise expectation too high.

Fully aware of the 'honeymoon period' some businesses experience, Robin and Gerard were wary that their initial success would wane. Yet in an impressive first year the company managed to make a net profit of about £20,000 after salaries and the bank had been paid. This was ploughed back into the hotel as working capital and went towards much needed equipment and stock, which was not included in its initial tight budget. Fortunately it proved such a popular niche in the market that during its early existence, the hotel was very busy. When problems did occur, Gerard believes the pair had quickly become strong enough to overcome them without letting them jeopardise the business.

Gerard recalls that to begin with they were careful never to overestimate how full the hotel would be to the bank manager. By being conservative with their estimates, it was not too difficult to beat the projected figures, and therefore be deemed a success. Gerard warns that 'if you plan to be busy from day one, you do not leave any possibility for problems'.

Complementing Expertise

Gerard's flair on the restaurant floor also improved the hotel's reputation for good service. He brought integrity to the wine side of the business, which became a unique selling point. His wine expertise gave the hotel a twist; putting the 'Vin' into Hotel du Vin. Robin's job was to exploit this from a marketing perspective and make sure it worked financially. With 20 years of experience in the hospitality industry, Robin felt comfortable heading up the business side of things: he had previously worked at The Berkely in London, The Elbow Beach Hotel in Bermuda and Hotel du Crillon in Paris, as well as his eight years at Chewton Glen.

However, the roles were by no means rigid. Both men were challenged to learn new skills from each other. Though Gerard was more comfortable on the floor, Robin learnt from him and was soon able to take over his position in his absence. In the same way, Gerard initially found the financial, administrative side of business pretty daunting, as he was not used to the pressures of everyday managerial duties. On one occasion, while Robin was away, one of the room's showers stopped working. Gerard was studying for his Master of Wine examination at the time and the last thing he needed was to have to mend a leaky shower when he could be spending his weekend studying ('tasting') wine. Although Gerard struggled with the business side of things, he rose to the challenge and subsequently completed an MBA course.

'Spend time nurturing and training your staff. Particularly the first ones.'

Upon opening, Robin and Gerard were joined by a few staff from Chewton Glen and acquired more local staff as their reputation grew in Winchester. They also tried various methods of recruiting staff such as advertising in local French magazines. Gerard notes that it is important to 'go down different roads' and not be rigid in your approach to finding suitable employees. Robin advises any boss to spend time nurturing and encouraging, training and retraining your staff. Particularly the first ones, in order to create some sort of ethos and identity in the business.

Their primary aim was not to create the chain of hotels that eventually emerged: believing it far better to ensure the first venture was a success before embarking on

The bistro at Winchester.

a larger scale expansion of the concept. Robin recalls their first business plan made 'a very vague reference to the fact that if this went well, there could be others,' and Gerard believes to aim for five or six hotels at the start is dangerous as you are focusing more on achieving goals than making your first business a success. In order to succeed, he says, entrepreneurs need to be ambitious but also remain grounded. Thus, it was only after the hotel in Winchester was firmly established and they were confident in their product that they contemplated opening another.

Vintage Advice

Robin and Gerard believe that one of the reasons Hotel du Vin became so successful was because of the detail that went into planning the business, something which they both aim to repeat. Robin believes that 'all good businesses are about managing the detail. Hotel du Vin was a great detailed business.' The founders encourage new businesses to watch early expenditure. It is pretty difficult to regain money once it has been spent, so Robin advises that 'being cautious and thrifty to start with is a good discipline'.

In 1997 the second Hotel du Vin was launched in Tunbridge Wells, but was not a foregone conclusion. Interestingly, Robin and Gerard explored the possibility of creating another hotel with the same shell but with a different unique selling point, such as a Hotel du Sport. Yet after some consideration and failed attempts at securing property, it was decided to continue with their winning formula. A consideration, which they took into account, was that a Hotel du Vin group would one day be much easier to sell than a collection of different hotels. Having always had a vague plan for exit, the expansion of Hotel du Vin into a small chain of seven hotels by 2004 was a natural progression that the founders took their time to achieve.

The founders do not believe that creating a chain of Hotel du Vins has compromised the emphasis on unique service. Gerard admits that he and Robin had wanted the chain to remain small, they should have stopped at two or three hotels. Once there are more than five, it becomes a group and there is nothing stopping the creation of more. Therefore, when the property company Marylebone Warwick Balfour (MWB) bought Hotel du Vin for £66.4 million in 2004 and continued expanding the chain into Scotland and other northern cites such as Chester, the founders supported this progression.

WHERE ARE THEY NOW?

Robin Hutson is currently the chairman of the exclusive London and New York members' club Soho House and is involved in a hotel in the South of France. Gerard Basset is using skills learnt at Hotel du Vin coupled with his MBA and is opening a hotel with his wife in the New Forest, with the same emphasis on his love of wine.

MWB are expanding Hotel du Vin still, opening branches in Cambridge, York and Cheltenham in 2007 and in Newcastle and Edinburgh in 2008. MWB also owns Malmaison, which was founded in the same year by Ken McCulloch who also recognised the niche in the market. They have continued in the same vain that Robin and Gerard began.

innocent
little tasty drinks

Innocent Drinks

Coming to Fruition

Company:	**Innocent Drinks**
Founders:	**Richard Reed, Adam Balon, Jon Wright**
Age at start:	**All 26**
Background:	**The three founders met at university and were engaged in various ventures together there. After working for a number of blue chip firms they decided to embark on their own business together**
Start year:	**1999**
Business:	**Fruit juice drinks**

I nnocent Drinks, which almost single handedly introduced the smoothie to Britain, is now one of the fastest growing drinks brands in Europe, with revenues of £78 million in 2006. The company, started by three friends, has amazed the business world by successfully launching a preservative-free healthy fruit drink and maintaining its ethical principles, despite its founders having no real experience in the sector. Innocent now employs more than 180 staff and has five offices across Europe. The company's offices are among the most friendly and relaxed in the world and its staff are extremely well treated, with perks ranging from free snowboarding trips to bonuses for having children.

Quitting the Rat Race

Three friends, Richard Reed, Adam Balon and Jon Wright, met at university and often worked on mini-business ventures together. Club nights were a speciality; Richard and Adam organised the nights while Jon designed posters and flyers to attract the crowds. Without realising it, the students were honing promotional skills which would be useful later. Also, they were learning that a sense of fun and enjoyment were important aspects of how they wanted to work. They often talked about running their own company together, although the idea of fruit drinks wasn't to surface until much later.

A selection of Innocent smoothies at their annual Fruitstock festival in Regent's Park.

After university, all three entered the world of big business; Richard worked for advertising agency BMP, Adam went to consultants Bain Associates and Jon worked for management consultants McKinsey and then Virgin. Like so many involved in the 'work hard, play hard' culture of the UK's capital they felt that their diets were far from healthy. At that time, 'juice bars' were opening up in London, offering different blends of fruit, sometimes also involving yoghurt and ice. It struck the three friends that they couldn't be the only ones who wanted something healthy each morning, as they made their way through the arduous commute. They came up with the idea of a healthy drink that could be bought off-the-shelf, solving the problem they had all experienced of waiting for ages queuing up at a juice bar. Furthermore, they wanted to make something that was totally natural, containing just fruit – no ice or water, let alone preservatives, stabilisers or any other chemical agent.

They began creating their own fruit smoothies at home, and eventually came up with some recipes, which they thought tasted great. Their first was strawberries and bananas, a variety that still sells well today, which was based on a 'communal love of these fruits'. However, with no real experience in making fruit juices or in the soft drinks market, they didn't know whether the product would sell.

'They asked customers to tell them whether or not they should give up their day jobs to start a smoothie business.'

They knew they needed to do some market research. In the summer of 1998, the lads decided to open up a smoothie stall at the 'Jazz on the Green' festival in West London that Adam and Richard had been running for a few years. Next to their stall they placed two large empty bins, one marked 'Yes' and the other 'No'. They asked customers to tell them whether or not they should give up their day jobs to start a smoothie business by putting their empty bottles in the appropriate bin. The crowds voted overwhelmingly for them to start a new business, so Jon, Adam and Richard left their jobs.

At this point, they hadn't thought of the name Innocent. While the jazz festival crowds had backed their drinks, they also overwhelmingly rejected the first trading name of 'Fast Tractor'. Other efforts: Naked, Fresh Inc, Fresh and Thirsty were also discounted before the trio decided upon their name.

'We went through thousands of different names, all the different variations, it was a case of getting the thesaurus out until we came up with Innocent,' Reed says.

The now famous logo was produced by a startup design agency called Deepend in return for a stake in the business. However, the company went out of business before Innocent went into production, so they never had to give up any of their shares.

Budding innocence

Almost immediately problems beset the plan; there was a massive amount of work to do and the three founders were soon shocked at how tough it could be to set up a new business.

> 'We were hopelessly naïve. We stopped working with just a month's pay to keep us going, but it was nine months before we were up and running.'

'We were hopelessly naïve,' Richard recalls. 'We stopped working with just a month's pay to keep us going, but it was nine months before we were up and running.'

As with many startups, raising money was one of their major early key obstacles. They needed to raise money to buy fruit and bottles and get the smoothies made. Bankers and investors were not as easily impressed as the crowds at the festival and shied away from the proposition. There were three overriding factors that the potential investors just couldn't ignore. Firstly, Innocent had no experience in the sector and appeared to have underestimated the complexity of food manufacturing. They had only ever made small quantities of their juices but were looking to expand across the nation. Also, their additive-free healthy offering had a very short shelf life, which meant that unless the product was sold quickly it would go off, which left investors fearing that they might end up owning a lot of rotten fruit.

Finally, it was the late 1990s and the investment world was caught up in a dotcom bubble, which had yet to burst. Everybody was trying to make money out of the internet and nobody was looking to back a fruit juice company. 'I remember hearing about lastminute.com and thinking 'oh my God, that is such a brilliant idea', and for one minute I was thinking "we should do a dotcom,"' remembers Richard.

Having left their high-powered jobs behind, the world in which the Innocent founders lived was now a harsh one. 'It was a case of our friends buying us the occasional pint and eating cereal three times a day. We come from great families but

Innocent staff at Fruitstock.

they aren't so rich that they could support us to that extent. The business very nearly never happened.'

Straining to Succeed

In one final, desperate move Richard sent out an email entitled 'Does anybody know someone rich?' to everyone they had ever known. The email was passed around and, via a former work colleague of Jon, it eventually landed in the inbox of a certain Maurice Pinto.

Pinto was a wealthy American with a lot of experience in investing in new companies. People like this are often referred to as business angels, as they are often the saviours of businesses' ideas, investing money and time to help grow young companies.

Adam, Jon and Richard went to see Maurice and, despite being close to 40 years younger than him, they got along very well. Maurice liked their business plan, and thought that Innocent addressed an important need: he knew that in the US there was a huge demand for smoothies, but the UK still had no real smoothie companies at that stage. The maverick in Maurice also found Innocent's unconventional approach to business refreshing; the trio had high ideals about how the company should behave towards its staff, suppliers and the environment. Maurice was impressed that they didn't rush into decisions and would always debate very heavily before coming to a conclusion, which they had to do because the business has no single leader. Their answer to Maurice's first question 'who's in charge?' was 'we all are'. In short, Innocent was determined to break the mould in every respect. While this frightened off some investors, in the end Maurice decided to invest £250,000 in return for a 20% stake in the business. Now, the company could really get going.

While they had been looking for funding Innocent had also been attempting to find a manufacturer and this had been no easy process either. 'We went around virtually every drinks manufacturer and they were all saying that we needed to make our smoothies with concentrate. However, we responded by saying that we have tested this and consumers don't want drinks made from concentrate, they want something natural,' Richard says.

Just like with the potential investors, they were turned down again and again. Manufacturers insisted that Innocent needed to use concentrate to make its drinks but the lads knew there was a demand for their natural product. Prior to gaining the funding, they had given small batches of their drinks to shopkeepers for free for them to sell on, as a market test, and the response was overwhelmingly positive.

'The shops wanted to place orders but we had to say "sorry, we're not really ready yet,"' Richard recalls.

The quest for a manufacturer eventually brought them to a small family business which agreed to make the drinks the way they wanted, provided that Innocent provide them with the machinery to do the production. Getting the manufacturing of the smoothies just right is far from easy, and today Innocent smoothies continue to win taste tests over other brands, so Innocent keep their manufacturer's identity secret. But that small family business is still making smoothies for them to this day.

The funding from Maurice came through in early 1999 and Innocent launched later that year with three recipes: strawberries & bananas, cranberries & raspberries and oranges, bananas & pineapples.

'Supermarkets don't even return your calls at first, then they say no and then if you are persistent you get a chance.'

To start with Innocent sold its drinks to high-end food retailers such as Harvey Nichols and Harrods, and to what was then a small coffee chain called Caffé Nero. These were Innocent's 'beacon outlets' though the big retailers were soon to follow. Waitrose was its

One of Innocent's DGVs (dancing grass vans).

first supermarket buyer: 'Supermarkets don't even return your calls at first, then they say no and then if you are persistent you get a chance. When we managed to get in front of Waitrose they could appreciate the drink was just right for their audience.' After Waitrose came Sainsbury's, and shortly after that all the big retailers began stocking their drinks.

From April 1999 until the end of the year Innocent had sales of £400,000. In its second year of trading, turnover hit £1.6 million, then £4.2 million, £6 million, £10.6 million, £17 million, £37 million and in 2006, £78 million.

The founders were able to draw on their professional experience to set strong foundations for the growth of the company. They made sure that they established strong relationships with suppliers as they viewed them to be vital for their success. They also planned ahead and considered where they would be in a year's time.

The company also literally framed its values, which have governed the way it has operated to this day: be natural by keeping it human and by using 100% natural fruit all the time; be entrepreneurial, chasing opportunities and challenging the status quo; be responsible, doing what you believe to be right; be commercial, think clearly and act decisively and be generous when offering praise to others and with charitable support.

A peak inside Fruit Towers.

WHERE ARE THEY NOW?

All three founders are all still fully involved in the business, which has expanded across Europe. 'Fruit Towers' in London is still the company's HQ although the company has offices in Ireland, Denmark, France, the Netherlands and Germany.

The trio have stuck to their ideals and have built a closely-knit, friendly and ethical company; the drinks are still preservative-free, the plastic bottles are 50% recycled and renewable fuels are used when possible. Staff retention is one of the highest in the world; of more than 200 people taken on, just 13 have left in eight years of trading. Maurice Pinto is still the only outside investor, although the company has turned down numerous offers of investment and to sell since becoming successful.

And, of course, the business has sold ever-growing numbers of drinks and has become a household name and much respected brand. In 2007 Innocent expects to bring in revenue of over £115 million for the first time; a significant achievement for any company, but even more so for one that has kept its ideals intact.

Cobra Beer

The Expertly
Brewed Brand

Company:	**Cobra Beer**
Founder:	**Karan Bilimoria**
Age at start:	**27**
Background:	**Chartered accountant and law graduate**
Start year:	**1989**
Business:	**Premium lager producer and retailer**

f you like eating curry at Indian restaurants, as most of us in the UK do, you will almost certainly have come across, and probably drunk, Cobra Beer. It is today by far the most dominant brand of beer at Britain's many thousands of Indian restaurants, being served in 90% of the 6,000 which serve alcohol. Less well known is that it also has a rapidly growing presence outside the UK, and particularly India. Its founder, Karan Bilimoria, was honoured in 2006 with a peerage, making him Lord Bilimoria of Chelsea.

Through the Bottom of a Beer Glass

Like many business initiatives, Karan's inspiration for the business came from dissatisfaction with existing products; as a 19-year-old student from India studying in the UK, Karan found Britain's beers too gassy and harsh to accompany Indian food. An English friend introduced the teenager to the national treasure English ale, and he was hooked. Yet this smooth bitter was too heavy to accompany food. From this conundrum, Karan decided the answer was to make a beer to his specifications; envisaging 'all the refreshing qualities of a lager' but a drink smoother and less gassy, so as to also appeal to ale drinkers while accompanying spicy food. His great grandfather had started a liquor business in India from scratch, so Karan would be following in his footsteps.

At first Karan put his idea to one side while he read Law at Cambridge and went on to become a chartered accountant at Ernst & Young. After completing his accounting studies in 1988, aged 27, he decided to obtain some business experience by importing goods from India. The son of an Indian army general and from a wealthy family, it is easy to assume that Karan had an inheritance to finance his business ideas, yet this was not the case. Grant-funded to study in Britain, he emerged £20,000 in debt. Yet this did not dissuade him from pursuing his business idea, which he'd been thinking about now for some years.

Karan wanted his authentic brew to be produced in India and exported to Britain. Today, investment in India is rapidly growing, but when Cobra started, it was very rare, mainly due to challenging legal issues. (Just two years later things changed substantially, setting off India's economic expansion and liberalisation.)

With beer production as the ultimate goal, Karan and family friend Arjun Reddy imported various items for about nine months. After bringing back some sample polo sticks from a Cambridge polo tour Karan played on, the friends formed A&K International Ltd, found a manufacturer in India and successfully persuaded their first customer to pay for half of their consignment up front, enabling Karan to visit India to oversee the manufacture of the sticks. The pair then managed to get Harrods to place an order and eventually sold 300 to the store. Although this business had proved

Karan and Cobra staff load one of their vans.

successful, it was not very lucrative, so the partners dabbled in other commodities including pearls, towels and silk jackets.

'Karan envisaged a global business, despite being in debt with no money to his name.'

While contemplating importing seafood, they stumbled upon an Indian brewery with its own seafood division in Bangalore. Mysore breweries, a former Coca-Cola bottling plant, was the biggest privately owned brewer in India, producing a popular Indian brand. The brewery did not, however, export its beer. The Indian brand already in production did not meet Karan's explicit criteria, so he convinced the brewery to make a new lager to his specifications, and to use his chosen branding. Even at this stage, Karan envisaged a global business, despite being in debt with no money to his name, and wanted to keep ownership and control of the brand name rather than simply distribute someone else's product to the UK.

An early Cobra bottle label.

Karan and Arjun were fortunate to have an experienced mentor to guide them through the starting up process. Arjun's uncle introduced them to his local bank, and from an old-style, trusting bank manager, the business partners got an overdraft facility of £7,000. Karan puts this down to the bank manager's trust that as a chartered accountant, he would be careful with money. Ever since this first loan, he has ensured finances are prioritised.

Having found a brewery to supply the beer he wanted, Karan and his partner hurriedly set about finding a way to sell it in the UK, signing a deal with some experienced people from established breweries in Britain.

'Never, ever go forward with an idea without actually testing it out on the consumer first.'

But at this stage customers could have been ordering 'Panther' beer. Having decided on this as his brand name, Karan travelled to India to oversee the production of the beer and labels at the printers while his partner stayed in Britain. But two weeks before bottling, Karan received a call from his partner: he and the distributors had been trying to pre-sell the beer, but no one liked the name. The partners could either ignore public opinion and continue with the name, or resort to their second choice, 'Cobra'. Thankfully, the labels hadn't been printed yet, so Karan used his brother's advertising agency to quickly re-brand the beer. This dramatic change so near production inevitably delayed the project and cost extra money. Yet as a result, Cobra Beer was born and Karan learnt a valuable lesson: 'never, ever go forward with an idea without actually testing it out on the consumer first'. So why 'Cobra'? Short and punchy, the name 'takes you back to India, without doing it in an obvious way', says Karan. The brand name is a huge factor in beer sales, so getting it right was crucial.

Punching Above Your Weight

The first five years of Cobra's life were the most difficult. In June 1990, as their first batch of beer arrived in the UK, the worst recession since World War II began. Karan describes the slow start as 'a jet aircraft, fully laden with fuel, on the runway. You know your plane should take off but it just doesn't lift off the ground. You have to persevere and stick with it until it finally takes off.'

Karan's family in India started to worry that despite his qualifications, he was becoming an "import-export wallah". Karan saw Cambridge friends and accountant colleagues earning high salaries at big investment banks, and he knew that he needed to focus on his product and his vision.

'Karan knew that to succeed they would need to punch above their weight.'

In Britain, beer is big business, and long-established, wealthy brands dominate pubs and bars. Unable to compete with their marketing budgets, Cobra's only chance was to promote itself as different, focussing on its smoother, less gassy character. Even with this distinction, Karan knew that to succeed they would need to punch above their weight, and with a clear strategy. Cobra's was simple – they had identified a niche market, the Indian restaurant trade. With over 6,000 Indian restaurants around the UK, all potential clients, this was a significant market, and one the bigger brands weren't focussed on.

From a standing start, Karan's sales approach was to visit as many Indian restaurants as possible and convince them to buy a crate of Cobra. Sometimes visiting as many as a dozen restaurants in one lunchtime, this was gruelling work. Karan carried the beer crates in his battered green Citroën 2CV, which they had to push start most days. The founders used to park a little way away from the restaurant they were selling to, so that the owners couldn't see the sorry state of their premium beer's delivery vehicle!

An early problem the partners faced came in the form of glass beer bottles. In India, beer is sold in larger, 660ml bottles that are recycled and used again. To start with, the Indian brewery producing Cobra would only use these bottles, while British restaurants only sold small bottles or draught beer. The brewery promised to consider producing smaller bottles once Cobra became successful. Turning this potential obstacle into a strength, Karan started selling this as a sign of the authenticity of the beer, and persuaded restaurants that it would help them sell more beer by

The Cobra 330ml bottle.

encouraging sharing. Cobra's larger bottles are a major part of its brand identity, and have now become so established that nearly all major beer brands are now available in the larger size bottle.

To New Heights

At the start of 1991, Cobra was being stocked in around 100 restaurants, already exceeding Karan's early estimates. The partners approached Ghandi Oriental Foods, the biggest distributor to Indian restaurants in London, and secured a lucrative deal for them to distribute Cobra to their restaurant customers. Now, the young business needed to find a way of funding the larger quantities of beer, as Ghandi would take sixty days to pay them. Using his accountancy knowledge and purchase orders from Ghandi, he managed to set up a form of trade finance, borrowing enough money from a bank to pay the brewery for the new, larger deliveries. The deal with Ghandi doubled Cobra's sales.

By 1993 the company's continued growth meant that it needed to raise £250,000. With the help of his accountant, Karan used the government Small Firms' Loan Guarantee Scheme to borrow £50,000, and – literally the day before his wedding – found a business angel who invested the other £200,000. Karan had offers of all the money from a venture capitalist, but did not want to take the money since the VC wanted one third of the company's shares for the money. By borrowing some of the money and finding a business angel, Karan was able to raise all the money the company needed without having to give away as many shares.

Cobra's first year turnover was approaching £300,000, but this steadily grew so that by the fifth year, revenue hit the £1 million figure that many businesses view as a sign of success.

BEST BEFORE:
You try anything else.

Next time you're buying beer, here's something to think about.
At the 2006 Monde Selection World Quality Beer Awards, Cobra won an incredible 12 Gold Medals. That's more than any other beer in the world.

Unusual thing, excellence

Cobra 'Best Before' tube advert from a recent campaign.

' Never give up, never ever give up. '

Karan valued Arjun's support as a business partner and so after he had left he set about building a management team. Karan is quick to attribute the growth of Cobra as a consumer brand to the first-rate advice he received, both from his own staff and his advisors. In 1996 Cobra introduced premium Cobra glasses to its restaurant customers, which helped double turnover that year.

However as a result of this growth, 'our problems also doubled' recalls Karan. Demand for the product was so high that in 1997 they had to move the brewing process to the UK to ensure quality and availability. Although a huge task, Karan says that this was 'the best move I ever made'. It took six attempts for the UK brewery to perfect the Cobra recipe, and the same one continues to brew the beer today.

If you asked Karan for advice, it would be, 'if you can, build a brand'. Begun from grass roots, Cobra has a very strong foundation that it could capitalise on when it had the money to invest in branding. Yet before this, Cobra's reputation was cultivated by word of mouth, giving the business a firm basis that no amount of marketing budget could create. Karan was careful to make sure that he never commercialised the brand when opportunities for expansion arose, as this would potentially alienate loyal customers. Now, as Cobra expands globally, Karan asserts that the essence of the brand, Cobra's character, must be maintained.

WHERE ARE THEY NOW?

Today, while still running the now substantial Cobra business, Karan Bilimoria also lectures in the UK and abroad, covering entrepreneurship, business, education and the Indo-British relationship. He is one of two Visiting Entrepreneurs appointed at Cambridge University.

Cobra has also started to sell wine, targeting the 35% of Indian restaurant clients who choose wine with their curry. The selection of wines have been named after Karan's father, General Bilimoria and not surprisingly have been developed to go well with spicy food.

Cobra beer is becoming increasingly mainstream, and is stocked in an increasing number of pubs and bars. The company recently added Cobra 0.0% alcohol-free, Cobra Lower Cal and King Cobra, the world's first double-fermented lager, to its range, and has won many awards for its brand as well as its beers.

Bebo

A Social Phenomenon

Company:	Bebo
Founders:	Michael and Xochi Birch
Age at start:	35 and 33
Background:	Insurance and online ventures
Start year:	2005
Business:	Social networking site

When social networking site MySpace sold for a whopping $580 million in July 2005 and YouTube followed suit for a mind-blowing $1.65 billion in October 2006, critics in the UK asked how and why the US had managed to steal the show. The thing is, they were wrong and their children could have probably told them why in one word: Bebo.

Bebo is a UK based 'social networking website,' similar in nature to sites like MySpace. While many might still not be familiar with it, in the UK more people now visit Bebo's website than visit the BBC online or Amazon. The site has signed up a staggering 28 million members in its first 18 months.

So just how did Michael Birch, the site's founder, create such a phenomenon? 'By giving people what they want and not giving them something they don't want,' he answers simply, 'and by not being greedy'.

Network Knowledge

That sounds simple enough, but Bebo's success was also the result of a long process of trial and error for Michael. Since quitting his IT job at an insurance company, Bebo was Michael's sixth venture. Three had failed, two were moderate successes and Bebo, of course, has been a total smash. For him, it was a completely natural process.

'Just because something fails it isn't necessarily a complete waste, you learn what you can from it.'

'It took about three years of trying before three years of success,' he says. 'It's a learning experience but just because something fails it isn't necessarily a complete waste, you learn what you can from it, realise one element that works well, and leverage that into a new business.'

Michael's ventures were all online. He knew from an early age he wanted to start and run his own business, and the arrival of the internet provided the impetus, and more importantly, the platform he needed.

'I was always entrepreneurial,' he insists. 'But I was trying to be entrepreneurial within a very boring insurance company and it was probably the most frustrating thing in the world. Then the internet happened and I quickly realised this was the

Michael Birch.

perfect medium to be entrepreneurial – and I already had half the equation because I understood the IT side of it.'

Stumbling Upon Success

Michael had experienced success with one of his earlier websites, BirthdayAlarm.com. This is a diary alert site that reminds you of key dates by email, to stop you forgetting people's birthdays or anniversaries. Once this was up and running successfully, Michael started experimenting with online social networks.

'Online social networking' is the new phenomenon that has taken the world by storm, and in particular people under the age of 25; for those that don't know what this means, it involves a website where anyone can register and set up their own profile page, telling anyone who cares to notice what they like and dislike; members can talk to each other, and use their likes and dislikes to find other people like them to talk to online. Some sites allow registered members to load photos and video clips of themselves, or things they like, onto their own pages. Social networking online forms a large part of what is now being referred to as 'web 2.0', a term covering a new generation of websites which offer far greater interactivity than witnessed in the first generation of the internet.

'I was fascinated with the first social networks such as Sixdegrees.com,' he says, 'and had ideas on how that content could be improved. We designed a social network in 2003 called Ringo.com.'

Ringo proved an instant success to the point that Michael and his team were unprepared for its growth. Aware of this, he decided to sell – just three months after starting it. 'We just couldn't afford to throw resources at it, we'd had three offers in a week and it was the hot property of the time,' he recalls. 'It was the second biggest social network next to Friendster. We decided to sell and focus on other things we were running at the time.'

The Birth of Bebo

Michael had to let Ringo go, but he wasn't finished with social networking, which was continuing to build momentum as household internet connections approached, for the first time, a critical mass. 'They were still early days for social networking, but I started to see how people interacting with each other could integrate with other types of media, such as music and video and how whatever suddenly becomes hot – at the moment it's blogging – fits easily into it. I found it completely fascinating that people were connecting in such a positive way and thought it had immense power and endless opportunity.'

> '*I started to see how people interacting with each other could integrate with other types of media.*'

Having played around with a number of emerging social networks, Michael sat down with a blank piece of paper to produce what, in his eyes, would be the ultimate network. It emerged initially as a photo-sharing network, but quickly evolved into a broader social networking site by the time a non-compete clause from the sale of Ringo had expired.

Standing Out From the Crowd

Michael was aware he had to enter the market with a unique proposition. For him, it was to address the youth market with a product that matched their user demands and understood exactly what they did, and equally importantly did not, want from a network host.

Initially that meant not excluding anyone by being too niche. 'We always intended Bebo to be a broad social network,' says Michael. 'Where there were niche verticals such as YouTube, we always wanted Bebo to be for everyone.'

That also meant not being too complicated or as feature-heavy as some competitors. 'It's designed to be simple to use. You can register, get a homepage and be up-and-running in minutes. There is a depth of features that a power user would want, but you don't need to use them. Other sites put people off by being too tricky.'

The second fundamental issue for Michael was to create an environment to harbour and encourage a network – something he insists is key to the member numbers Bebo has attracted. 'It's about trying to encourage a healthy community without trying to dictate how that community behaves,' he explains. 'We control things such as pornography otherwise that would just escalate, but we won't delete things because we think it's silly. If you want to create profiles for your dogs and cats, that's fine by us. We've been very careful about using the right language, treating people with respect but making it light-hearted and fun.'

'If you're too corporate, the social network society will backlash against you.'

It might sound obvious stuff, but Michael insists it was these subtleties of product that made Bebo standout from the crowd of emerging social networks. The internet-savvy youth market can be a harsh critic and Michael placed far more emphasis on providing the right environment than on an all-singing, all-dancing design. He insists that Bebo's modest aesthetics and simple functionality, in addition to its very limited advertising spaces, and casual moderation, was fundamental to its creditability.

'It was absolutely crucial that we weren't too corporate,' he says. 'If you're too corporate, the social network society will backlash against it. They don't want a corporate feel or for a large corporation to be running it.'

Guerilla Marketing

Not being 'too corporate' meant mass advertising was a no-go. Successful social networking sites tend to evolve on their own merits – not because a billboard and a million flashing banner ads say it's a great place to visit. For most cash-starved startups void of marketing budgets that's great news, but it's also a major test of product too.

'It's almost impossible to contrive a natural-feeling social network by driving people there,' says Michael, drawing the comparison that Milton Keynes was a perfectly conceived city that nobody wanted to live in.

As a result, there was almost no launch advertising or promotion for Bebo when it went live in July 2005. 'I threw a link up on BirthdayAlarm.com for, I think, two days, then we took it back down,' says Michael. 'So we literally just seeded it with the first few people and then it just grew on its own.' And boy did it grow.

The Cost Behind the Craze

In terms of initial startup cost, Michael already had two technical programmers working for him on a freelance basis and insists that the launch site 'didn't cost that much'. Initially, his and co-founder, and wife, Xochi's wages, in addition to the programmers' fees, were just covered by BirthdayAlarm.com profits.

Aware that growth could be brisk from his experiences with Ringo, Michael also invested in new servers to support the anticipated new traffic. But Bebo was quickly in a position to support the purchase.

'Within a month it was generating revenue from advertising,' says Michael. 'It took another month for that money to come through, so within eight or nine weeks it was cashflow positive.' There are a number of agencies which sell advertising for other people's websites, and Bebo used these to sell advertising on its site, which kept their costs low and meant that it was someone else's job to do the selling, freeing Michael up to concentrate on building the site. Michael also used a widely available software product to 'serve' the adverts to their site, rather than trying to create it from scratch. Using these off the shelf products and services enabled Bebo to start far faster than had it done everything itself. This also allowed them to sell advertising in different countries even though they were only based in one – which was important since Bebo soon had substantial numbers of users all over the world.

Until January 2005, he and Xochi remained the only employees and even after the first full-time employee arrived, it was six months before another did; however the business then grew to 28 full-time staff within a year. In such an extensive period of recruitment, Michael found it difficult to find skilled employees suited to the company.

'To us, 28 feels like a huge company, but in reality most of our competitors have between 100-400 people, so it's still pretty small and that makes it really important to find the right people.

'It's been challenging and difficult. It's just difficult to know if someone is any good – their CV can say they are, but are they really? Google interviews people seven times, and while we're not that crazy, recruitment and interviews is something we focus on.'

Michael is also passionate about maintaining a small business culture as Bebo gets bigger. 'I absolutely never want to become or behave like a corporate and we try very hard to ensure it's an exciting business to be involved in, and we give stock options, which obviously people are excited about.'

Michael's ethos has been to grow organically. His vision still, he insists, is to spend money as it's made and recruit staff only when needed. However, in May 2006, he took the enormous sum of $15million of venture capital from Benchmark for an undisclosed slice of equity. Michael is adamant, though, that nothing's changed.

'We were cashflow positive at the time and we haven't spent any of the $15 million,' he says. 'We raised it because it's good to have a cash buffer even though you're profitable. It does give us the ability and confidence to grow aggressively when we need to, without having to get the finance to do so first.'

Michael's frugal approach isn't profit driven, however. It's all about 'growing in the right way' – indeed, he's passionate that Bebo shouldn't be generating anywhere near as much money as it could be. From day one, the business plan has been to make 'a little bit more than we're spending' and nothing more.

Advertising is Bebo's sole revenue stream – but Michael insists long term success and wealth is better achieved by nurturing it, not exploited it. 'People do get annoyed if it's overly intrusive so we've never done pop-ups or pop-unders and we only have a maximum one ad unit per page,' he says. 'Clearly we could make a lot more revenue in the short-term by throwing more advertising at it, but in terms of growing a community that wouldn't be right and people wouldn't react well.'

> 'We're aiming to make money, but not as much as we possibly can.'

'We're aiming to make money but not as much as we possibly can. The aim is to grow the business and we think we can do that more quickly by not being greedy and ultimately we'll then have a much bigger business that we can then make more money from.

Instead Michael is focussed on being one of the key players able to offer a quickly emerging alternative to traditional online advertising formats. Rival network and US No.1 MySpace has agreed a number of headline-making advertising deals with the likes of Fox and Google and Michael is more than aware of the power of his site as a window to the youth market. Product placements, branding campaigns, TV exclusives, and music promotion are all on the cards, but in a format that's friendly to users and exciting to advertisers. Positioning Bebo to take advantage of such opportunities in the long term is far more important to Michael than cleaning-up now on banners.

'Ultimately it is all advertising,' he admits, 'but advertisers are always looking for new ways to reach people and while banner advertising works very well, engagement marketing is becoming increasingly popular. Placing ads outside traditional ad units helps it get noticed and then people also don't think of it as advertising.'

Looking Back

Bebo's membership figures today are incredible, yet the company is just 18 months old and it's only fours years since Michael was still banging his head in frustration on his insurance desk. Michael's rise might seem the ultimate entrepreneurial success story, but he's quick to point out that, back then, quitting his job felt like a very real risk.

'I told Xochi I'd do it for three months and get a job if it didn't work – and it took three years. In hindsight if I knew everything I knew now I could do it a lot more quickly, but sometimes that's the best way to do it.'

Michael also insists he wouldn't have got to where he eventually has if it wasn't for his determination not to be deterred by failure – three times. Ultimately however, he insists it was a combination of this and the ability to let go of a stumbling idea that let him move forwards.

'You need to know when to quit. We could have spent our lives on three websites that might never have worked. Quitting one idea shouldn't de-motivate you.'

WHERE ARE THEY NOW?

Bebo is now the largest social network in the UK, Ireland and New Zealand. It is number three in the US, and two in Australia. It has 28 million registered users, and is number one, even in the US, for time spent online per member.

Time will tell just how big Bebo can get or whether Michael Birch ever monetises it to the extent he and many analysts think he can – or whether it becomes the next web 2.0 mega deal. Michael insists there's no plans for an exit, but at the same time dismisses the MySpace and YouTube deals as the 'steals of the century', so what price Bebo we might ask? Whatever Michael decides to do with Bebo, it is clear that it's a major force and growing all the time.

PizzaExpress

Inspired by Italy

Company:	**PizzaExpress**
Founder:	**Peter Boizot**
Age at start:	**35**
Background:	**Sales, teaching, journalism and street selling**
Start year:	**1965**
Business:	**Pizzeria**

PizzaExpress is sufficiently well known that it needs almost no introduction. Today it operates 350 pizza restaurants in the UK and Europe, and has made several entrepreneurs justly successful and famous. In 1965 when Peter Boizot opened the first ever PizzaExpress, its future was much harder to predict.

Peter returned home from a stint working and travelling in Italy but couldn't find even a slice of pizza anywhere in England, let alone a pizzeria. Convinced of the potential, he swiftly set about changing that.

Culinary Inspiration

Peter's taste buds first sampled pizza in 1948 when his headmaster dispatched him, aged 18, on a three-month foreign exchange programme to experience life with the Uzielli de Mari family, in Forte dei Marmi near Pisa, Tuscany.

Pizza was a favourite in the Uzielli de Mari household and soon became equally admired by its enthusiastic guest. Peter, repulsed by blood and the slaughter of animals, at the age of five had turned vegetarian and had subsequently grown-up on a bland variation British staple meat and boiled veg, minus the meat. Discovering pizza was a revelation.

In Peter's *PizzaExpress Cookbook*, written in 1976 (Penguin Group Ltd), the founder expresses, 'It was colourful to look at, fragrant to smell, succulent to taste,' he recalls. 'As a non-meat eater to eat a pizza with mozzarella with tomato on a pastry base with an olive or two was just up my street. The pizza became, from that moment, a food which was to nurture my body and my pocket for many years to come.'

After completing his National Service in Egypt and studying History at Cambridge University, in 1953 Peter seized the opportunity to live abroad again. A short spell teaching in Paris was followed by a period working for Nestlé in Switzerland, while a move into sales took him to Germany and on visits across much of Europe before he made his way back to Italy and its capital, Rome.

Here, Peter first showed his entrepreneurial flair, which he insists was always part of his genetic make-up, combining work as a journalist for the Associated Press with selling souvenirs and postcards to tourists from a barrow in St Peter's in Vincoli Square. Long, tiring but enjoyable days were rewarded with heady nights of pizza and wine. Peter was in heaven.

Deciding to Go it Alone

Eventually the pull of home and the nagging conscience to pursue a career took him back to England, but he was determined not to leave his love for pizza in Italy for a second time – or at least that was the plan.

'Back in England, I just couldn't find a pizza – not even the Italian restaurants did them.'

'Back in England, I just couldn't find a pizza – not even the Italian restaurants did them,' he insists. Driven by a yearning to live life as an individual and a reluctance to work for someone else, Peter decided to solve this problem himself.

'Sick of them not existing I thought "why don't I open my own place?" So in 1965, that's what I did.'

Starting Up

Peter's mantra was authenticity. He wanted to make, sell and, yes, eat real Italian pizza, albeit made in the UK.

The first job was to buy a proper Italian pizza oven – and there was only one place to start. 'I flew to the home of pizza, Naples, got in a cab and said "take me to your local pizzeria",' recalls Peter. 'There I was sent to meet Signor Notaro, a manufacturer of ovens, who agreed, for £600, which was a lot of money back then, to send it to England along with an Italian chef to work it.'

PizzaExpress' first restaurant in Wardour Street, 1965.

Aside from an authentic oven, the other 'essential' was real mozzarella. Shipping from Italy every week in the 1960s was unrealistic, but Peter tracked down London's only mozzarella producer and agreed a deal for exclusive supply – and a whole lot more than he'd originally bargained for. The deal didn't just secure Peter an unrivalled cheese supply, but also the now great PizzaExpress name and his first premises.

The mozzarella factory was owned by Margaret Zampi, widow of the late film director Mario Zampi, who several years before his death had unsuccessfully tried to launch a pizza restaurant, named PizzaExpress, on Wardour Street in London's Soho.

'He'd done everything properly. It was the ideal setting, he imported an oven, even set up a cheese factory,' says Peter. 'However, movie stars craved more luxurious food and unfortunately Zampi, with his simple pizza, was ahead of his time.'

Zampi eventually caved in, undertook an expensive refurbishment, changed the name to The Romanella and began offering standard Italian fare. Despite initial success, The Romanella had fallen on hard times following Zampi's death and was on the verge of liquidation. Peter saw it as an opportunity, however, so he borrowed £100 from a friend, Renee, and made an offer to acquire the ailing company from the widow.

'She was most helpful and she agreed to sell me the shares of PizzaExpress Ltd,' says Peter in his much loved cookbook. It's since proved a fine investment of course, but at the time, he wasn't so sure. 'I took on the staggering task of repaying creditors £14,000. It seemed a lunatic deal,' he admits.

Pursuing the Italian Vision

'We started by cutting large pizzas into eight slices and giving them away on grease-proof paper through the front window.'

Despite securing the keys to 29 Wardour Street, a prime location at the centre of London's nightlife and dining, it was to be months before Peter opened. In a decision he was later to at least partly reverse, Peter decided there was no need for the plush décor of The Romanella in a modern pizzeria and set about ripping it all out. However, with insufficient tools and labour, or money to pay for either, it proved a frustrating and turbulent process.

To make matters worse, Peter's one tonne Italian oven made it across Europe and over the channel but was never going to fit through the front door, forcing them to knock down a sidewall to accommodate it. Confused at holding paintbrushes instead of spinning dough, Peter's Italian manager left and his imported chef handed in his notice. Peter had to act fast, and swiftly found chef Rino Silvestri, from Naples, to step in.

'Peter's one tonne Italian oven made it across Europe and over the channel but was never going to fit through the front door.'

When the first PizzaExpress eventually opened its doors, trade was slow. 'Only people who had been to Italy had tried pizza and it was obvious my idea was not properly understood by the denizens of Soho,' he says. 'We started by cutting large pizzas into eight slices and giving them away on grease-proof paper through the front window. People loved it and would walk by shouting, "Ahh, pizza pizza!" but when we started to charge (at two shillings (10p) a slice), business began to wane.'

Peter was fiercely determined to persevere and rejected calls by onlookers and well-meaning advisors to supplement his menu with more familiar British favourites, such as chips and sandwiches. He opened before lunch and didn't close until four or five in the morning, picking up trade from the late night drinkers who stopped by for a slice.

Adapting the Business Plan

While he flatly refused to compromise on his pure pizza vision, eventually Peter was persuaded to revise his business plan. Ronald Simson, a friend from Cambridge and City banker Peter had turned to for investment, suggested they move slightly up market.

'I had this romantic rustica idea of selling everyday-life Italian food served up on grease-proof paper or paper plates. However, it's a difficult economic base to grow from as people stay a long time and spend little. We didn't have a nice enough décor to attract higher reaches of Soho, so Simpson suggested we should trade up a little.' Together with Simpson, Peter was able to raise enough money for this improvement.

For the redesign, Peter turned to Italian designer Enzo Apicella, who, ironically, had fitted out The Romanella Peter had ripped apart. Later Enzo worked on 85 PizzaExpress restaurants and was responsible for designing its famous art nouveau logo and 'PizzaPizzaPizza' window pattern. In came a wine menu, dining tables and simple but attractive furnishings – the first restaurant to resemble the format we all now know and love.

The upgrade drew in Soho's diners and pizza quickly became more than a mere street snack. Overcoming one further obstacle of seeing off a neighbouring competitor and eventually acquiring it, Peter embraced the attention of becoming London's latest culinary hotspot using his status as host to entertain press and cement his reputation as something of a local celebrity and to get PizzaExpress known to the masses.

The contemporary design of PizzaExpress at London Wall in the City of London.

Express Expansion

Within three or four months, the relaunched PizzaExpress was bringing in a healthy £2-3,000 a week in sales. Peter is proud to have brought over the first Peroni beers from Italy, as he approached the manufacturer in Naples and asked to sell it in his pizzeria in England.

A second restaurant followed 18 months later in a former dairy factory on, Bloomsbury's Coptic Street next to the British Museum. Peter says that this step is never easy for any business, but the company adjusted and expanded accordingly. Enzo again designed it with a remit to replicate the aura of the first PizzaExpress but with a completely unique design and décor.

This became a feature of PizzaExpress' roll-out with Peter as determined to avoid becoming a homogenous and faceless chain as he was to grow the business. His first ambition was not to create the chain that PizzaExpress is today, but to succeed at one or two restaurants at a time, although he admits it had occurred to him that the concept may well grow.

'*I saw the PizzaExpress company as a necklace with each restaurant being an individual and unique gem.*'

'I always loathed the idea of a chain,' he says. 'It's well documented that I saw the PizzaExpress company as a necklace with each restaurant being an individual and unique gem. Each time we opened a restaurant we added a gem.'

The Coptic Street restaurant was the first to feature original artwork on the walls and live jazz, something which, along with the deliberate sourcing of unusual and unique buildings, continues to set both PizzaExpress and its individual restaurants aside.

The first two years of PizzaExpress also saw Peter introduce his personal invention, the Pizza Veneziana, to the menu, with a percentage of every one sold going to the 'Venice in Peril Fund'. More than £1 million has been raised and Peter has been formally honoured by the Italian government by way of thanks, as well as receiving an MBE at home.

Roll-out

Expansion followed steadily and then rapidly throughout the '70s, '80s and early '90s through traditional roll-out and briefly a franchising model, as the nation quickly developed a hunger for a food unknown to its shores just decades before. For most of this time, the business was generating more cash than it needed to grow, so little extra finance was required. Peter acknowledges, though, that he was fortunate to have a 'generally helpful bank' and that his original investor Simpson remained an active investor for many years.

The opening of the 50th PizzaExpress restaurant on South King Street in Manchester in the 1980s stands out to Peter as his proudest moment. 'It felt like a real achievement,' he says. 'Like we'd finally become a big company.'

Peter eventually sold his shares to the PizzaExpress company in 1993, a group consisting of David Page's G+F holdings, Star Computers (a front company for Luke Johnson and Hugh Osmond) and Matthew Allen. Since then the company has been floated on the stock exchange, taken private again, and made fortunes for the three now well-known entrepreneurs, Johnson, Osmond and Page. The company is currently owned by more recent competitor ASK Pizza & Pasta – but Pizza Express remains the market leader in the UK.

Peter believes the one thing that made PizzaExpress work is what keeps it successful today: authentic Italian pizza. In the foreword to The PizzaExpress Cookbook, he quips: 'Those who have sought to change the original Italian images of the pizza receive my condolences for not being able to think of a name for their products, because it sure isn't pizza the way God intended it!'

Entrepreneurial Vision

Looking back even to the earliest days of struggle and sale by the slice, Peter is adamant he never doubted the potential of pizza or that he was the man to introduce it to the UK public's palates.

'The world was my oyster! I believed I could go as far as I could,' he insists. 'I liked doing my own thing and so took well to being my own boss. I don't regret anything, and wouldn't change a thing.'

WHERE ARE THEY NOW?

Peter Boizot has since gone on to own other businesses, including restaurants, hotels, retail property and Peterborough United Football Club, as well as becoming heavily involved in the jazz scene, starting the Soho Jazz Festival. He also played hockey competitively until into his late 60s!

Now, at the age of 77, he's just as passionate about life, business and PizzaExpress as ever. 'I'm not involved on a day-to-day basis anymore and it's not my company, but I am its president,' he says. 'They pay me a salary still and if they want my advice then they know where I am!'

Dreams

Live Your Dreams

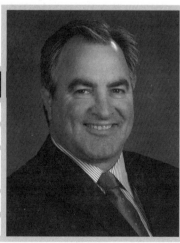

Company:	**Dreams**
Founder:	**Mike Clare**
Age at start:	**30**
Background:	**Area manager in furniture retail**
Start year:	**1985**
Business:	**Bed retailer**

Mike Clare opened his first furniture store in Uxbridge in the summer of 1985, scraping together the money to get started. He always had 'big plans' for the company that began life as The Sofa Bed Centre. But in the 20 years that have passed and after some serious re-branding, such plans have surely been eclipsed by a much more successful reality. Dreams has won Furniture Retailer of the Year three times, turns over £160 million a year, and as it continues to grow, Dreams is now firmly established as Britain's leading bed specialist with more than 150 bed superstores nationwide.

Reviving a Dormant Idea

'*It was his gut feeling which ultimately spurred him on.*'

Mike had been thinking of owning his own furniture retail company for a long time before he decided to leave his job as Area Manager at a local furniture store to start his own business. It was, he says, not a new idea and he had in fact even entered into talks with people 'way back before that' in the late 1970s, before realising he did not have enough of a business credit rating, funds, or in fact the trust of his landlord to forge ahead. As a result, the idea lay dormant for the next five years before Mike decided, shortly after his 30th birthday, to take the plunge and start up a company that specialised in selling sofa-beds.

According to Mike, a key business consideration is to have a good speciality product to focus on and sofa-beds seemed to fit the bill nicely at that time. They were a new product, freshly imported from America and 'all the rage' amid the general market in the 1980s days of 'hopeless and uncomfortable' bed settees. They had also, he says, not yet been widely picked up by other retailers, which he discovered by scouring furniture shop adverts in places such as The Yellow Pages. It seemed an opportune time to develop this niche. While admittedly 'risky', Mike confesses that it was his gut feeling which ultimately spurred him on for he had a strong belief he was meeting a demand in the market and his business could be a real success.

From Fledgling to Fighting

Every business needs money to get started, and Mike initially struggled to come up with the funds he needed. Calculating that he would probably need somewhere

The Sofa Bed Centre's exterior, 1985.

Branching into beds.

between £20,000 and £25,000 to fit out a shop and gain suppliers, he approached the bank to see if they could lend him the money – to which he was told that they would match whatever he himself could raise. As Mike remembers it, this totalled about £8,000: £2,000 from the sale of his car, £2,000 worth of savings and a £4,000 loan charged to his credit card – ostensibly for refitting a kitchen! Consequently, the initial funds that he had to invest in his own business were £16,000; at least £5,000 less than he had initially hoped. Although disheartening, Mike was far from put off. Today, he says, if you are starting up a business you must be determined to make it work no matter the difficulties or obstacles in your path. While many people, he says, seem deterred by the idea of taking a risk, if your house is on the line and you are really planning to put everything you have in, then you will, in fact, do 'whatever's necessary to make it work' and not be confined by difficulties, financial or otherwise.

'You must be determined to make it work no matter the difficulties or obstacles in your path.'

After securing a loan, the next stage was to find a cheap property to lease as The Sofa Bed Centre's showroom. In April 1985, he found an old motor-parts store in Hillingdon, which he bought. It was cheap he remembers because it was in a 'terrible state'. Although he had originally only intended to buy a small, single store, the landlord who leased the property also offered the property next door saying the two together would only be 50% more than the initial rent. As a result, Mike ended up leasing both and knocking a big archway between the two; something

Dreams' Rhapsody bedstead.

he was glad of as he later found even the combined measurements were 1,000 sq ft too small!

After initiating the buying of his property, Mike went to local libraries and looked in directories to find sofa-bed suppliers. He then rang them and asked if they would be happy to supply a new furniture business in a local area. Although there weren't many main suppliers of sofa-beds, Mike ran into a common difficulty: the suppliers he spoke to were extremely reluctant to do business with a new company, due to the risk that they wouldn't get paid. However, using his initiative and persuasive personality, he eventually found one company which not only offered to supply him, but also offered much support including a new set of supplier names for him to work from. Mike's experience suggests that slightly exaggerating the truth can sometimes pay off – by pretending to be a much larger company, he managed to gain lots of useful contacts and information! Ultimately his hard work and enthusiasm paid off, and a month before the opening of his store, Mike had eight willing suppliers.

Now all he needed was customers. Mike believed strongly that his showroom was the key to attracting customers, and so he spent 18 hours a day there 'doing everything'. He enlisted the help of family members and Annette who did the bookkeeping and finances, who he found through an advertisement in his shop window before he opened.

'You need to be willing and able to solve problems whatever it takes.'

Before opening he worked hard cleaning, re-carpeting, placing spotlights, receiving and displaying stock and pricing items. The pressure was on to open and to start taking money quickly, so Mike scheduled a 'Grand Opening' for mid-May, just a few weeks after taking possession of the store. Mike expected, naively with hindsight, that this would be the first day for everything, including trade. As a result, he was convinced that everything had to be perfect for that day. Mike remembers fondly that the day before the opening one of the last things to arrive was a doormat – which Mike had ordered to replace the oil-stained one that had been left. But when it arrived, it didn't fit in the concrete with the door opening over it, and so refusing to be beaten he spent the night on his hands and knees, chiselling the concrete down himself! Although amusing now, it is typical of the dedication every new business needs if it is to succeed; there simply was no alternative since the shop had to be ready for opening the next morning. When running a small business successfully you need to be willing and able to solve problems whatever it takes.

It was finished in time, and the next morning Mike was shaking hands with the Mayor in front of the local press and his newly opened Sofa Bed Centre. He was lucky in that word had spread about the opening of the store. He had 'bigged it up' so much that images from the opening were even featured on the front page of one of the local papers the following day. And even more importantly, the shop made ten sales that day!

That was when the next problem became clear – delivery and storage. Mike was using a local van man to deliver the orders but it was a few weeks before he realised that he couldn't fit all the stock he was having delivered into the showroom. To overcome this he managed to rent some space in the back of a nearby industrial unit to store the sofa-beds until they were due to be delivered to customers. This is typical of Mike's approach to business – addressing each problem as it crops up and focusing on it determinedly until it is solved.

The sales carried on, with the first month's reaching an impressive £30,000; and the first year's sales were £400,000. In 1985, this was far more than a normal shop. Mike generated enough profit to finance the opening of a second store that November. After the experience from his first store, Mike made sure the next was much bigger and had its own storage area out the back to make delivery much easier. Landlords need to know that their rent is going to be paid, and usually look at a prospective tenant's 'covenant' which means its reputation and ability to pay; once a business has lots of shops it is easy for landlords to check that other landlords are being paid on time, but for new businesses this is obviously not possible. The fact that The Sofa Bed Centre was now trading made it far easier to persuade the landlord to accept Mike as a tenant for the second shop. Having a second property meant expansion thereafter was much easier; as a result sales continued strongly. By the end of the second year, The Sofa Bed Centre had expanded in to five stores.

During one of Mike's monthly meetings with key staff, the limitations of The Sofa Bed Centre were discussed. To Mike, sofa-beds seemed too much of a niche product and he wanted to expand into selling something else. According to him the 'obvious' product to sell alongside sofa-beds was either sofas or beds – and beds seemed the natural answer; they were an easier shape to fit in vans and as we all spend a third of our life in bed, the product appeals to everybody! Mike also decided to change the name of the company to Dreams Limited, a name which Mike likens to Virgin in that it doesn't mean any one thing and can be used to brand more than one product. He promptly registered the company and got ready to trade under the new name.

Problems

It was literally on the first day of trading as Dreams Ltd, in 1987, when the company encountered its next problem: an injunction, delivered by motorbike. Mike was told by the messenger that this injunction meant the company would have to stop trading under the name, Dreams Ltd, as there was another company called Dreams who were selling beds already. Mike managed to persuade the other business that both companies could trade as Dreams until a court case to decide who was allowed to use the name long term. Mike's Dreams fought this court case over a long time, trading successfully all the while, and eventually winning the rights by default after the other company went bust. From this point Dreams went from strength to strength.

Living the Dream

Since the beginning, Dreams' success has been swift, and surprising. Mike found that although selling beds did not bring in big money instantly, it is such a big market that it proved 'easier' than he had thought, with sales in the first week of the new name and range hitting £15,000 and quickly rising thereafter. Mike attributes this steady progression in part to learning from his mistakes. So while they bought some beds, which didn't sell or weren't sufficiently well-made early on, Dreams continually

The Dreams head office in High Wycombe.

adapted, changed and concentrated on putting things right. This willingness to change is key to many successful entrepreneurs. Eventually, even though they had begun by selling both sofa-beds and beds, beds began to do so well and took up so much room in the showroom that sofa-beds took something of a backseat, leaving Dreams focused on becoming Britain's leading bed specialist.

> 'Dreams continually adapted, changed and concentrated on putting things right.'

It is a reputation that Mike has been careful to cultivate and to maintain over the years, and all the evidence points to its success. Between 2002 and 2003 alone, Dreams increased its store tally by a third, totalling 100 stores and then expanded by beginning to manufacture some of its own beds and supplying to businesses such as nursing homes and hotels. Dreams is responsible for opening the largest bed store in the world, in the West Midlands, and now operates more than 150 stores in total.

WHERE ARE THEY NOW?

Mike Clare remains Chief Executive of Dreams and plays an active role in the company, overseeing all major decisions, including assisting a move into international franchising.

Since its humble beginning as The Sofa Bed Centre, Dreams now also has a successful website and has expanded its product range further into bedroom furniture.

Cotton Traders

A Whole New
Ball Game

Company:	**Cotton Traders**
Founders:	**Fran Cotton and Steve Smith**
Age at start:	**40 and 36**
Background:	**England rugby captains, worked in the sportswear marketing industry**
Start year:	**1987**
Business:	**Clothing distributor**

Former England captains Fran Cotton and Steve Smith teamed up in 1987 to provide quality rugby shirts via mail order as they noticed an increase in demand for casual sportswear that was not supported by retail companies. Now, Cotton Traders have more than 2 million customers on their database and enjoy an annual turnover of over £68 million. Fran and Steve were remarkably fortunate during the founding years of their company and benefited from great support that helped them tackle situations head on.

Rugby Roots

Fran and Steve met at Loughborough University where they were both studying for a joint honours Physical Education degree with Maths and History respectively. Their friendship extended into a partnership on the rugby field and the pair appeared together in numerous high profile games, playing for local clubs, the Barbarians and the British Lions. They excelled on the international stage and in the 1970s they participated in numerous tours with the England team, Fran captaining the team in 1975 and Steve in 1981 and 1982.

While a career in rugby may not be a standard entrepreneur's background, and taught the pair nothing about running a mail-order business, Fran believes it gave himself and Steve the people skills to succeed. They learnt, without being aware of it at the time, leadership abilities and motivation techniques that can be directly translated to the business field.

Fran and Steve were playing in the amateur era of the game and so both men also had full-time careers. Steve went into teaching and lectured in Physical Education at West Cheshire College. He eventually took a post with the Distributive Industry Training Board where he lectured in management and personnel issues. Fran also went into teaching until he began working as regional sales manager at the Royal Doulton Group.

Rugby shirts: Cotton Traders' first products.

After retiring from rugby, Fran and Steve were reunited, this time in the business field. In 1983 they joined Bukta Sportswear as account managers and within two years the pair had been made joint managing directors. When French Connection bought Bukta in 1985, Fran and Steve found that their new owners had very little interest in the sports division they had purchased and the pair became frustrated with the lack of interest French Connection showed towards their new developments. They felt they were principally running the sportswear independently, and only benefited from the financial contribution French Connection was making.

Rugby Shirts Down the Pub

Fran and Steve believed that their bosses did not understand the changes that were happening in the clothing market. In the mid-1980s, it had become fashionable to wear tracksuits and trainers for leisure. Fran remembers how his mates used to keep their old rugby shirts and wear them down the pub – this, he explains, was the real 'embryo' of the product. The initial concept was to market international rugby shirts as leisure garments, which, according to Fran, had never been done before in the UK; other companies had been selling rugby shirts as part of their sports division, but this was only a very small part of the overall retail market. Fran and Steve were to be the first to market rugby shirts to the general consumer as leisurewear.

While working at French Connection, Fran and Steve were invited to a business lunch with David Jones, then the chief executive of clothing catalogue Grattan. At the lunch, one of the directors present mentioned that a US company called J. Crew was making a fortune from the sale of rugby shirts in America. Fran and Steve began tracking this company's progress and their findings confirmed to them there was indeed a market for casual sportswear.

The founders then came across another American company, a menswear brand called Boston Traders. Inspired by this company, within ten minutes the founders had come up with a name for their venture. Using Fran's surname and the American company's wording, they came up with the simple yet effective brand Cotton Traders; 'it was that easy', Fran recalls.

'You need the advice of people who have 'been there and done it.'

In 1987, after two years of working for French Connection, the ex-rugby players decided to fly solo, create their own business plan and find investors to finance the operation. They approached the top drawer accountancy firm Arthur Andersen (no longer in existence) while they were still working at French Connection. They worked with them to put together their business plan. Fran argues this was one of the best choices they made while in the preliminary stages of the business. They were able to use excellent professional advice to create a quality business plan, which they could then pose to potential investors.

Fran emphasises the need for any startup business to receive sound business advice from experts. For Fran and Steve, David was 'a very important influence' especially in the formation and early development of the company as he provided a wealth of experience and was someone who the founders could 'bounce ideas off'. As Fran expresses, you need the advice of people who have 'been there and done it'. Writing a strong business plan also proved to be invaluable, as the first potential investor they approached 'jumped at the chance' to invest in their idea.

The founders had envisaged they would have to spend around three or four months presenting their plan to many different financiers, and were pleasantly surprised when a deal was made in a matter of weeks. The investor, 3i, the largest venture capitalist organisation in the country, quickly responded to their proposal and Fran and Steve snapped up the offer. Fran admits they could have 'hawked around' for a slightly better deal, but the offer on the table was fair and everyone was eager to make a start.

In total, the business needed £100,000 in startup capital. 3i invested £65,000 and the partners put in the remainder. They sourced their rugby shirts from a supplier called Matlock Textiles in Derbyshire who controlled all elements of production. Fran comments that this was the 'perfect supplier to be with to start off' as all the shirts arrived ready to dispatch and the founders played no part in the manufacturing of their merchandise.

Fran and Steve had their investment and supplier in place before they officially launched Cotton Traders on August 1 1987. They began the business from a very small unit next to Altringham Station, just outside Manchester. It contained some small offices and a little warehouse space: about 'a couple of thousand feet' in total.

In the opening week they promoted their new business through two advertisements. The first was printed in *Rugby World*, a specialist rugby publication. Fran was sure they would be inundated with orders straight away from this advertisement, so he drove to the post office to pick up the sacks of mail – the postman handed him only three envelopes. They realised that as this publication was sold from the magazine shelf over several weeks, orders from the advertisements would take longer to come through. However Fran and Steve experienced a very different reaction to their

Fran Cotton in his rugby playing heyday.

second advertisement, which appeared in *You* magazine, a supplement in the *Mail on Sunday*. Fran remembers he was at the office at 8am that Sunday but was so overwhelmed with calls by 9am that he had to call Steve, who brought various friends along to help man the busy phones.

Described by Fran as an 'instant touchdown', this advertisement turned out to be 'one of Cotton Traders' most successful ads of all time'. The initial advertisement in *Rugby World* also came up trumps eventually and generated a high level of interest. By the end of the first week of trading they had received 1,500 orders, which was a 'hell of a good start', and by the end of the second week this figure had doubled. Since the initial advertisements had proved to be so effective, they decided to place further advertisements in a variety of publications in order to widen their customer base. As they had predicted, Cotton Traders filled a gap in the market for casual sportswear which major retailers had sidelined.

Initially, Fran and Steve ran the business themselves but it soon became obvious they would need to employ staff to manage the influx of orders they were receiving. In the few months between the launch of Cotton Traders and the Christmas period, Fran and Steve recruited five or six full-time staff to organise the dispatch of their product. Fran believes that these first employees had to be people who did not mind taking a risk by working for a newly established business.

'Without that passion, you are going to fail.'

Cotton Traders had an impressive first year, turning over around £1.5 million, which, Fran agrees, from a 'standing start' is very good – Fran and Steve were both very aware that many new ventures fail in the first year. Fran believes Cotton Traders were one of the businesses that succeeded because they began with a 'bloody good idea' that no one else had thought of. He also notes that by being passionate and 'believing you can successfully put your idea into practice', a new business will increase its chance of success; he warns that 'without that passion, you are going to fail'.

A Whole New Ball Game

After the initial success of the rugby shirts, Fran and Steve wanted to make sure sales did not wane, 'because early on it is about survival'. In the second year of the business, they looked to expand the range of products Cotton Traders were offering and began investigating silk products that were being sourced from China. Fran and Steve decided to approach NEXT with an offer of a joint venture; however, when Steve arrived at their offices, he ran into their old acquaintance, and advisor, from Grattan, David Jones who had by now been made Chief Executive at NEXT. He told Steve they were wasting their time trying to sell his buyers their silk product but directed them across the road to a marketing company called Kaleidoscope. There, the Marketing Director recognised the Cotton Traders' brand and told Steve to drop the silk idea. Instead, they worked on a joint venture catalogue, as Kaleidoscope was part of the Grattan mail-order group which also owned NEXT.

Talks started with Kaleidoscope in late 1989 and Cotton Traders developed their 'expansion' ideas and decided to continue to broaden their range, but stay within casual leisurewear. With Kaleidoscope, they were able to move from selling just one product to a wider range in a catalogue with expert support. Within three or four months of entering negotiations with Kaleidoscope, Cotton Traders launched its first catalogue providing a range of casual leisure wear, ranging from their well-known rugby shirts to chinos and denim wear. They switched suppliers from Matlock Textiles and were able to use NEXT's established supplier base due to Kaleidoscope's links to Grattan.

Cotton Traders grew steadily throughout the first few years of the company, and were able to buy out 3i's stake by 1990, becoming totally independent with no outside investment. While this is impressive, Fran admits the fast expansion of Cotton Traders meant the company struggled internally and with hindsight, he feels that they should have expanded in a more controlled way. He notices that they were so keen to develop the business that their infrastructure could not keep pace with their marketing. Therefore, for a short while, Cotton Traders struggled to keep up with demand and deliver the level of service that it aimed for. Eventually, the company introduced and

Fran and Steve with a Leicester Tiger's shirt.

established more effective systems and increased the number of personnel so that it could stay in step with the level of interest its marketing was generating.

The partnership with Kaleidoscope lasted three years until Grattan was sold to Otto Versand, the biggest mail-order company in the world at the time. At this stage, Cotton Traders brought the production of its catalogue in-house and from 1991, Fran and Steve controlled every aspect of the company themselves. Cotton Traders now entered 'a whole different ball game' as Fran describes.

This step meant they had to find bigger premises, hire more qualified staff and set up an infrastructure tailored for Cotton Traders. Fran remembers that the next two years were 'probably the most difficult period of our business' as the kind of expansion the company was undergoing meant that they were 'sailing pretty close to the wind' until they had established the new expanded structure.

'Get as much capital as possible behind you, so you can ride over any storms – because there will be some.'

Cotton Traders succeeded at achieving this significant company development through 'grit and determination'. Aware that every business will inevitably hit difficult patches, Fran deems perseverance an essential attribute for entrepreneurs and believes problems must be approached with determination and tackled in a sensible way. He advises a new business to 'get as much capital as possible behind you, so you can ride over any storms – because there will be some'.

In 1997, Cotton Traders continued their close relationship with NEXT plc, which acquired a 33% share in the company. David Jones was appointed Chairman of Cotton Traders, acting as the representative from NEXT. He has since retired from NEXT but is still employed by Cotton Traders as both Fran and Steve greatly value his input and contribution to the business.

WHERE ARE THEY NOW?

Still very much involved in the day to day running of Cotton Traders, Fran Cotton handles the mail-order operation while Steve Smith runs the company's wholesale division also appears as a commentator for TV, radio and in the press.

Cotton Traders is approaching two decades of business and is today the UK's fifteenth biggest online clothing retailer. With £4.5 million annual profit, Fran describes 'we are now in a position, and have been for a number of years, where you can plan ahead and expand in a controlled way'. Their aim is to become a first-class, multi-channel business, with a strong catalogue, strong website and strong store presence – Cotton Traders now has over 50 stores throughout the country, opening its flagship store in Cheshire Oaks in April 1988. Rugby clothing only accounts for 2% of the company's sales as Cotton Traders have expanded into the retail market, becoming the UK's sixth biggest footwear retailer, with the introduction of a range of larger sizes, up to 5XL.

Codemasters

Mixing Business
with Pleasure

Company:	**Codemasters**
Founders:	**David and Richard Darling**
Age at start:	**20 and 17**
Background:	**Schoolboy game makers**
Start year:	**1986**
Business:	**Computer games publisher**

Richard and David Darling were dubbed computer whiz kids when they set up Warwickshire based computer games company Codemasters at only 17 and 20 years of age in the 1980s. The brothers started out with a hobby, and went on to create a multi-million pound business. Their healthy obsession at first led them to make best-selling games for other publishers, but this naturally progressed into the founding of their own company.

The company is one of very few to have ridden the waves of growth, boom and slump successfully in a turbulent industry which has proved too much for many businesses. Still owned by the Darling family, Codemasters has just celebrated its 20th anniversary and is now one of Europe's best-selling and most profitable game-makers. Codemasters has had a staggering 64 UK number ones.

Growing up with Gaming

Given their background it is perhaps not surprising that Richard and David became entrepreneurs. From a young age, their childhood environment was full of electronic gadgets and corporate business ideas: their grandfather taught them to wire a radio and build small machines while their father, an entrepreneur himself, was creating the world's first disposable contact lenses which he eventually sold as a successful business. David describes how they had always been 'comfortable' with the idea of running their own business, and so when they discovered the relatively new world of computer technology their imaginative minds started racing.

Their interest in computers began when they were nine years old and living in Vancouver. David recalls that they used to stay late after school to experiment with the school machines. From here their fascination with technology erupted and soon after, their father bought a Commodore Pet on which his sons created their first game, *Dungeons and Dragons*. The brothers spent much of their time experimenting and creating versions of games that had swamped the gaming arcades of Canada, enthralled by the new technology. When Commodore launched a new computer, the Vic 20, in America, a friend of the boys, Michael Heibert, bought one, and the boys increased their knowledge and thirst for gaming. They then bought a 'machine code emulator', which was hard to learn and use, but let them make much better games. There were very few games around, and those on sale commercially were expensive, so the Darling's versions became instantly popular among their friends at school.

David felt that the school system was not very sympathetic to gaming as a profession, 'we knew if we wanted to make games for a living, we'd need to start our own business'. So they created their first company in 1981 with Michael, naming

'We knew if we wanted to make games for a living, we'd need to start our own business.'

it Darbert Computers, an amalgamation of their names. However in 1982, shortly after its inception, the Darling brothers were sent to school in Britain to live with their grandparents. This did not perturb the teenagers who continued to send each other copies of their games. David describes this first venture as 'more of a business plan' as Darbert Computers, as a working operation, never came to fruition; it was only on English shores that their first trading company began.

As their entrepreneurial spirit blossomed, later in 1982 the brothers formed Galactic Software Co. Ltd and aimed to take their hobby one step further. They saved up enough money to advertise in *Popular Computing Weekly*, a leading magazine for computer game fans, scrupulously saving the £70 needed to advertise from the weekly £5 their mother used to send them from Canada for lunch money. This initial advert worked, and the Darlings received an impressive response, making their money back in no time.

At this stage, very few shops sold games, so the brothers posted the games (on cassette tape) to customers who wrote in with an order. At first, the brothers used to buy blank tapes and copy the games themselves, but soon the demand became too high so they used a music duplication company nearby to make larger quantities for them. David recalls how he thoroughly enjoyed his later teens, zooming around on his motorbike collecting tapes, dropping off the program code of new games and most of all, the thrill of creating new games.

The brothers when they worked with Mastertronic in 1985.

Understandably, the Darling's schooling took a back seat to the booming business. David stayed and finished his 'O' levels, but Richard left school before his to concentrate on the business, but still showed up to sit his exams. They each gained five 'O' levels, though none of them in computer science. At first, their father James longed for them to go to university and continue their education, yet this changed, as David remembers, 'once we showed him the potential of the technology, he was hooked'.

Teaming up to Break the Mould

Drawing attention to themselves for all the right reasons, within a year of operating this fledgling business, the brothers were headhunted by the ambitious new computer games company Mastertronic in 1983. Mastertronic wanted to revolutionise the computer games market then, by charging just £1.99 for their games, when most other games were sold for £5.99 or more; they were convinced they would sell substantially greater quantities of games at the lower price, and were looking for talented people to produce games for them to publish. They stumbled on two gems as the brothers began working for them as contract programmers. The first game the Darlings produced for them, *BMX Racers*, £1.99 on the Commodore 64 and Sinclair Spectrum, sold an unprecedented 250,000 units, helping establish Mastertronic as a force in the market.

The Darlings had 'great fun' writing as many games as they could for Mastertronic, also getting their friends and contacts to write games for them too. Realising that they were writing a significant percentile of Mastertronic games and with excellent contacts at their fingertips, the brothers decided to set up a development company called Artificial Intelligence Products, to work in partnership with Mastertronic. The deal was that Mastertronic owned half of this company and had the right to source all their games from AIP. David explains that 'really they were just buying back the right to develop their own product which AIP had the exclusive licence to'. Founding AIP put the Darlings in the driving seat.

The brothers soon realised they were, in fact, making more than 70% of Mastertronic's software and so, early in 1986, they negotiated to buy half the shares in the company – a staggering feat for a 17 and 19 year old, but one that reflected their value within the company.

Having worked with gaming companies for years, the Darlings were well aware that there was an abundant market in which they were becoming more and more influential. After three years working with Mastertronic, in March 1986 the brothers sold their shares for £100,000, which was enough to set up their own company. Six months later, they founded Codemasters.

Mastering Their Art

The brothers made an excellent team. David, the elder of the two, concentrated on the business side while Richard focused on writing games. Even now, roles are distributed to account for each other's strengths. With the backing from their entrepreneurial father, now back from Canada, and years of experience in the industry, the brothers' credentials were impressive, and unlike many startup businesses they did not have to find a bank manager to borrow money to set up the new company. David recalls their only concern was 'to create a product that the consumer wanted'. They began their operation out of their grandparents' house in Somerset, but quite soon this was no longer practical and Codemasters rented a business unit nearby.

'The brothers decided that they would, from the outset, lead the market as it changed.'

Codemasters aimed to produce quality budget titles in the same market as they had helped Mastertronic target. Mastertronic sold their games in places such as petrol stations and newsagents as well as multiple retailers such as WH Smith, thereby reaching a wider consumer audience than they would by solely being sold in specialist shops. Codemasters intended to echo Mastertronic's 'accessible' approach and capitalise on the now flourishing market. David believes business ideas need to be 'scalable', meaning they have the potential to expand if they first succeed. Codemasters was at the forefront of a rapidly growing and changing market and the brothers decided that they would, from the outset, lead the market as it changed.

In September 1986 Codemasters launched with 12 new games. While writing for Mastertronic, David had seen that sales figures were much better for 'simulators' compared to less realistic games, and the brothers also found they were also slightly easier (and apparently more fun) to make. Their first, *BMX Simulator* for the Commodore 64, went straight in at number one in the games charts and went on to become one of the world's best selling games of the time, selling 250,000 copies. The *Grand Prix Simulator* followed soon afterwards and repeated their initial success. Codemasters' first offerings helped them make a strong name for quality, top-selling products in the games industry.

The games were first sold in the independent computer shops that were prolific at the time and, after a few months, gradually became listed in WHSmith, Woolworths and Boots. This was relatively easy as there was a big consumer demand that the chains were eager to meet. Their father also had a friend who worked with a large electronic retailer who was a valuable contact for the company.

The Darlings were able to monopolise the budget computer games market as no other company solely released low retail priced games: the highest retail price of any Codemasters game was just £1.99. Despite their low prices, David made sure that the game quality was never compromised and so, with relative ease, Codemasters

David and his father, Jim Darling.

established itself as a reputable brand that delivered, and so it gained a following amongst computer enthusiasts.

As the cost of game production was kept at a minimum, Codemasters could afford to conduct a major advertising and marketing campaign. They brought in PR legend Lynn Franks (rumoured to be the inspiration behind BBC's satirical sitcom Absolutely Fabulous) who helped them to achieve a lot of national press coverage. Her job was made easy by the brothers' remarkable youth success story which captured the imagination of many headline writers. Enduring every possible play-on-words with their surname, 'the Darlings of the industry' had arrived at a time when entrepreneurs were all the rage. The brothers appeared on dozens of children's TV shows such as the legendary Saturday morning show *No. 79*. This amount of press coverage raised Codemasters profile enormously and was a 'great way to promote our games to the players'.

David describes how in business as well as PR, their youth was a real advantage to them – they had their 'finger on the pulse' and were able to empathise with the teenage consumers they were marketing to since they themselves had been these consumers just a few years earlier. Their youth, passion and enthusiasm injected energy into a business that needed exactly that to succeed. As David explains, 'it was a new technology, and a new market that required new skills'. Without youth on their side, they would have found it harder to reach their target audience. When occasional situations arose where their youth could have posed problems, David explains that they chose to ask an older friend or employee to front for them, thus overcoming the problem.

David explains that 'low costs, low margins, but high volume gave the business a lot of momentum' so that Codemasters enjoyed a fantastic first year: the company had become the best selling software house in Britain. And, as the brothers hoped, it had indeed established itself as a reputable, high quality, budget brand.

By the end of the year, there were around 10 full-time employees, writing and marketing the games, and many freelance game programmers working for the Darlings. From the start, Codemasters was very much a family affair. They sourced their first employees from their close family and friends – David's best friend Stewart Regan came on board, and another good friend of David's, James Fairburn, produced all Codemasters' graphics.

'You can't spend all day trying to make one perfect decision; you haven't got time to do that.'

While on the surface, Codemasters' startup looks a flawless operation, David admits they have had inevitable difficulties. Yet he agrees with a piece of advice a successful Jewish businessman once told his dad: 'If you are not making mistakes, you are not making enough decisions. David is a strong believer that business is a constant learning process – errors occur. He advises that 'you can't spend all day trying to make one perfect decision; you haven't got time to do that'. And all businesses, including Codemasters, encounter some problems; what matters is how these problems are dealt with. He perceives that one of the most important things a founder can do is to 'make sure you have enough good people to ensure that you are not just spending all your time fighting fires'.

After their initial success, the brothers were careful to ensure they grew – organically – and their benchmark was to ensure they made a profit every year. David comments that the most challenging aspect when founding a business is to constantly improve products to ensure you have something the consumer actually wants. Codemasters faced the challenge of keeping up with the fast paced technological developments of the late eighties and early nineties. They moved on to creating games for the then new 16-bit computers such as Ataris's ST and Commodore's Amiga, and then to produce games for the new dedicated games consoles that flooded onto the market. Eventually, Codemasters veered away from the budget market, as the cost of cartridges in the console market was too high to allow them to sell for such low prices.

By quickly and effectively reacting to ensuing developments in the gaming industry and producing some very successful series, such as the Micro Machines franchises, Codemasters continued to grow in size and prominence, and over the years have turned down numerous offers to buy them out.

‘It is not just about making money – it is also what you do every day so make sure you enjoy yourself.’

David acknowledges that their success is largely down to hard work. He remembers that during the first ten years, they used to put in a 'ridiculous amount' of hours. Therefore, in his opinion, to spectacularly succeed will require 'enormous amounts of dedication'. Because of this, 'it has to be something you love or else you are not going to be able to put the hours and energy into it'. It is vital to realise that 'it is not just about making money – it is also what you do every day so make sure you enjoy yourself'.

The Darling's passion for their industry is clear and Codemasters has adapted and developed alongside the technology that has boomed in the last ten years. David still exudes passion for his company, insisting, 'I love making games and I love commercial business – it's fun!'

WHERE ARE THEY NOW?

The Darlings continue to be heavily involved in the games development process. Adapting to the ever-changing 21st century technology, Codemasters currently programmes games for all current and next generation consoles, as well as PCs. This includes Microsoft's Xbox and Xbox 360, Sony's PlayStation 2 and 3 and Nintendo's GameCube and Wii. Recently top venture capitalist Benchmark has invested to help them grow to the next level.

Codemasters intends to market their games globally and now has publishing operations in the USA, Germany and France as well as the UK and Marketing operations in the Netherlands and Spain. David Darling has recently set up a MySpace account, where he is happy for people to ask him further questions about the Codemasters' story: www.myspace.com/daviddarlinguk.

Dorling Kindersley

Pioneers in Publishing

Company:	Dorling Kindersley
Founders:	Peter Kindersley and Christopher Dorling
Age at start:	33 and 34
Background:	Art Director and Cartographer
Start year:	1974
Business:	Publisher

With a fresh approach to publishing, Peter Kindersley and Christopher Dorling aimed to introduce heavily illustrated full-colour reference books into what was then a comparably dull market. Begun in 1974, the company's first year turnover reached almost £1 million, worth more like £7 million in today's money – a staggering amount for a new business.

Founder Foundations

Trained as a painter, Peter left home aged 22 to find his fortune in London. He worked for a small magazine publisher where he learnt the publishing skills which he would rely upon heavily throughout his career. He became Art Director aged 28 while working at publishing house Thomas Nelson and there met Mitchell and Beazley (who went on to found the eponymous illustrated reference publisher). Together they were heavily involved in the expansion of Thomas Nelson and built up a plethora of contacts. In 1967 Mitchell and Beazley set up with map publishers Philips, and Peter joined them from the outset as Art Director. The new company flourished but after five years, Peter began to tire of the founders' 'aggressive approach to publishing'. Discontented, he wanted to set up his own publishing house; he recalls that for him, 'necessity was the mother of invention'.

Peter's break away was not amicable, and Mitchell and Beazley attempted to stop him setting up a rival company by keeping him on in directorial status. Initially, Peter had to set his company up in his wife's name, as it was not until he had been released by Mitchell and Beazley that he could be named on the paperwork. Christopher Dorling, a friend from Mitchell Beazley, joined the new venture, known to the trade as 'DK', bringing his skills in sales and editing to complement Peter's strong visual skills. Christopher was also a very good 'numbers person', balancing Peter's imaginative mind.

Dreaming in Colour

They envisaged a publishing company that did not do 'one off' books but created a series spanning lifestyle issues from gardening and wine lists to children's books. The emphasis from the outset was on producing quality illustrated reference books, something attempted previously, but Peter and Christopher intended to 'step it up by a huge amount'. While text had traditionally swamped the publishing world, the entrepreneurs wanted to introduce more visually led, image focused books to create an informative, highly readable resource. With such rich illustration, the founders were aware of how easily the books would translate into different languages, and pursued international sales from the start.

'Peter and Christopher intended to step it up by a huge amount.'

Peter speaks of their unswerving devotion to produce quality books and the integrity in their intention. While some publishers were concerned with the size of their pay packets, Peter assures that he was never in it to make money. Naturally, he needed to make a living, but as he explains, 'I also had a genuine craft-like interest in the process and I just loved building and making books. I was very lucky – I got very well paid for it.'

DK was founded in October 1974 from the back room of Peter's south-London home. Immediately they took on Christopher Davies, one of the editors from Mitchell Beazley, who complemented the founders' skills. The three of them could lean on their reputation as some of the founding members of Mitchell Beazley, facilitating initial business, especially with contacts in America and Holland.

Initially, DK was established as a book packager, creating ideas for titles and acting as liaison between the authors and publishing houses. They would then sell the rights to various publishers, print the titles in a bulk run and the books would be published under the respective publishing companies' own names around the globe. By doing this, DK ensured a wider circulation of their titles than would have been possible had they set up as a small publisher in the UK alone. This was a relatively new approach and the founders relied heavily both on their reputations in the book trade and on the quality of their first few titles.

Peter on Sheepdrove Organic Farm in Lambourn, Berkshire.

At their inception Peter settled on three title ideas to launch with. Stemming from his own interest in evolution, he wrote to well-known author Nigel Calder and commissioned a children's book on evolution: from this, *The Origin of Johnny* was born. Confident that wine was a popular subject, they searched for an author and approached Pamela Vandyke Price who wrote for them

The DK building on the Strand, central London.

The Taste of Wine. Vandyke Price was already working with a publisher, yet left to work with DK as she was interested in illustrating her work more heavily, something which Peter recognises her 'reticent', traditional publisher did not offer. Lastly, renowned author John Hedgecoe was approached to produce *The Book of Photography*, another interest of Peter's. All three titles would be packed with diagrams and photographs in the heavily illustrated format that people have come accustomed to over the years. With three titles in hand, DK set to work creating sample page layouts with 'lavish designs and presentations' detailing every page of the books to aid persuading publishers of the innovation of their new approach.

Alternative Methods

Armed with these titles, Christopher and Peter attended the international Frankfurt Book Fair in October 1974, but could not afford a stall at the popular industry event. Instead, they set up in a 'very dubious hotel in the red light district' and sent their secretary to the fair to implore people to visit them at the end of their day. They spread the layouts on the bed and sat their visitor down on the only chair in the room to conduct their presentation. They received a small but significant turn out, with publishers visiting due to the founders' reputation, and also because of the innovative books DK were offering.

After the fair, due to the strong interest DK had received from publishers, the next step was to finalise the book contracts directly with publishing houses. Peter recalls that as they were well respected by groups of publishers in New York from previous business (Peter was the designer for New York publications *The Joy of Sex* and *Hugh Johnson Wine Atlas* – both huge successes), here was a logical starting point. With a simple business plan they persuaded the bank to grant them a £10,000 overdraft, by putting up Peter's house as insurance, to finance the trip to America. Peter remembers that they did not use all of this – indeed, the startup was mostly funded by £17,000 that Peter had been paid when leaving Mitchell Beazley.

'This break was the little bit of luck that is absolutely essential when starting a business.'

They arrived in New York with their preliminary titles and set about visiting numerous publishers. The first trip lasted three weeks, during which the founders camped out in a seedy Spanish hotel just off Broadway. In the weeks before Christmas, they finally sold all three titles to Random House, meaning they only had to complete one momentous deal. Peter describes this break as the 'little bit of luck that is absolutely essential' when starting a business. They had impressed with their experience, but also had ensured they had strong presentations and good authors behind the titles. On his return from New York, Peter received the news that he had been officially sacked from Mitchell Beazley, meaning he could legally now run the company himself.

Once the partners had secured their first major deal, they hot-footed it to Holland, Italy and other European countries to sell translation rights to publishing houses. The beauty of highly illustrated books, Peter explains, was they could easily be produced in several different languages: the illustrations stayed the same, and only the black plate had to be changed for the different language texts. Peter explains that it was essential to have the manpower to carry this process out and therefore, as soon as the first proofs of the book were ready, DK had foreign language speakers on the team to facilitate deals with foreign publishers. This was an excellent move as speaking the same language was 'such a huge advantage' and made it very easy for publishers to talk to them. In the first year, DK had employed a salesman who spoke five European languages and an excellent Spanish-speaking saleswoman while most English publishers perhaps had one person in sales who was bilingual. Quickly, DK had a sales force of about six people who would travel the globe completing deals.

To print the various different language editions together was a cost efficient method for the usually expensive illustrated books. The origination costs were one off and this was shared between all publishers' editions; a huge saving for heavily illustrated books. For example, instead of paying for their own print costs for 20,000 copies, each individual publishing house was part of DK's 120,000 print run and therefore benefited from the considerable discount generated by printing on this scale. This, Peter argues, was the 'key' to their business – spreading the cost of production over a large number of copies and being able to sell the illustrated books at a very competitive price. As the books were reprinted, the packagers ensured they used the opportunity to bring other publishers in on the run.

With some important deals in the bag, DK worked manically to complete the first publications. In order to do this, the company took on some freelance designers and editors, known from their time at Mitchell Beazley, so that in the first year of production, there was a team of around ten working on the books and dreaming up future titles.

Up in smoke

By mid-1975 the three initial books were ready for print and were sent to Van Leer, a print and reproduction company in Amsterdam, to print. It was in Amsterdam that disaster struck and DK received the biggest set back of their career. Soon after the material had been sent, there was a blazing fire in the Van Leer printing house; Peter remembers the 'amazing shock when the printer rang us up and said "all your artwork's burned to smithereens"'. For a moment, Peter believed DK was 'dead in the water'; the fire cost them thousands and all their hard work had literally gone up in smoke.

Fortunately, the photography had been saved, but all other work needed to be redone. Van Leer worked extra hard to print the books as fast as possible and Peter recalls both the publishers and insurance company were extremely sympathetic. Astonishingly, despite this major hindrance, Peter reports that the books arrived on time in America.

'All your artwork's burned to smithereens.'

Once published, the success of the three preliminary publications varied. *The Origin of Johnny* was sold to a number of publishers over the world but Peter remembers that overall it 'didn't work'; amongst themselves *The Taste of Wine* was dubbed 'The Waste of Time'; but *The Book of Photography* took off from the word go. It arrived at a time when the Single Lens Reflex cameras were emerging on the market and 'what you needed was a really good book on how to use them'. The author John Hedgecoe struck gold with his practical, informative blend of illustrations and tips. DK was the first to produce a highly illustrated, practical – 'but at the same time inspirational' – book on photography. Soon after its publication in spring 1975, companies such as Kodak were getting in contact. Peter describes the whole experience as 'fairly incredible' and without doubt sees the book as the best decision he ever made. This book went on to become a million copy seller and was re-published as recently as 2003 in a new and updated format.

From the preliminary titles, Peter estimates DK's first year turnover was just under £1 million. Peter describes the 'trick' the founders used to ensure steady cash flow into the company from the outset. Traditionally, authors had received small advances from their publishers to fund them while they complete the book. With an excellent reputation behind them, DK exploited publishers' expectations of paying such advances and asked for a third of the money on signing, a third when they showed adequate proof of the book's development and a third on delivery. As most publishing companies were used to giving advances, they embraced this approach and thus, DK avoided going into their overdraft or overheads exceeding income. Due to the success of the photography book, Peter explains how 'every time we sold another edition, we got money in. That basically made us cash positive so we could get on and come up with new ideas.'

Developing DK

A year after its foundation, DK moved to new offices in Covent Garden, central London, where it remained for the next 26 years.

'If you have an idea and everyone says it's mad, that's probably the idea to pursue.'

Within the next three years, the publishing house produced eight titles, three of which have gone on to become million copy sellers. These included *The Complete Book of Self-Sufficiency* by John Seymour, which aimed to inspire readers to respect the land, grow their own food and waste nothing. Peter explains that at first, the book was not well received, especially by the German publishers. No one could understand why they would need to know how to milk a goat or harvest crops and told DK they would not publish the book. However, Peter believes that 'if you have an idea and everyone says it's mad, that's probably the idea to pursue' so went ahead and published the book anyway in 1976. It became a best seller and sold over a million copies in Germany alone! Remarkably, thirty years later, Peter saw a copy being sold at a bookstand on a recent trip to Japan. This was also a book that greatly influenced Peter personally and inspired him to contemplate the effect he was having on the world around him, and has proved to be the inspiration behind his more recent endeavours.

DK's current Health titles.

Peter also saw a gap in the market for a well-illustrated baby book so sought out author Penelope Leach. *Baby and Child,* published in 1977 by Michael Joseph, was 'an instant success' and again achieved the balance between information and illustration.

DK's subsequent appearances at the Frankfurt Book Fair differed heavily from their debut. Riled by others pinching DK's ideas, the publisher created a wall around their area and patrons could only enter if invited. Peter recalls how 'people loved it, they felt they were superior'. Again, DK made sure all nationalities were made welcome with tables for each country with a native speaker hosting.

Momentously, in 1982 DK became a publisher in their own right in the UK. The first title created under the DK brand was a first aid manual entitled *The Red Cross First Aid* which went on to sell millions of copies in over twenty different languages.

After an extremely successful career, Christopher decided to leave the company in 1987 and pursue other interests. The year after Christopher's departure, Peter launched the well-known *Eyewitness Guides* to fill the hole in the market for exciting non-fiction children's books. Famous for being a leading children's publisher, there are now 150 titles in this series and the series has sold over 50 million copies worldwide.

In 1990, Microsoft bought into the company, boosting DK's net worth immensely. Peter remembers the first letter of interest he received from Microsoft and immediately knew 'this could be really important to us'. He knew this letter 'wasn't an ordinary letter' and urges entrepreneurs to 'take opportunities when they are offered'.

While the DK story is undoubtedly one of success, Peter admits he has made some mistakes along the way. Perhaps naturally, there are certain titles he wishes he had published but passed by. He regrets never publishing a 'Science Kit' (although one has since been published by DK) and recalls that passing up the opportunity to work with world-renowned wine authority Jancis Robinson was a 'big mistake'.

In 2000, an impressive 80% of all DK publications were still in print. This was the year in which Peter retired, after nearly forty years in publishing, following an ill informed decision by a company executive to over invest in Star Wars merchandise. Subsequently, the company was acquired by Pearson and now resides under the Penguin group umbrella. Under the stewardship of Gary June, DK continues to produce quality illustrated family reference and children's titles.

WHERE ARE THEY NOW?

Peter Kindersley has continued his quest for quality in his relatively new venture, an organic farm set in the Berkshire downs. Without possessing a farming background, Peter admits he is more interested in the organic farming sustainable model – of making food and at the same time preserving the environment. Sheepdrove Organic Farm works in partnership with Neal's Yard Remedies who provide organic skin care and remedies. The farm won the SEEDA (South East England Development Agency) Sustainable Business Awards in 2006.

MeetingZone

Simplifying
Doing Business

Company:	MeetingZone
Founders:	**Tim Duffy and Steve Gandy**
Age at start:	**47 and 41**
Background:	**Telecommunications**
Start year:	**2002**
Business:	**Audio and web conferencing service**

Following the horrors of the terrorist attacks in New York on September 11 2001 there was an immediate drop in executives' willingness to travel to business meetings. Around the same time joint partners Tim Duffy and Steve Gandy had an idea for a new business which has proved to be very good for them, their customers and shareholders. They identified a gap in the market for a new provider of collaboration services which took full advantage of new, web-based, technology. Focusing their attentions on creating a service that was fast and flexible, Tim and Steve launched MeetingZone in 2002, and it has grown rapidly, and with remarkable consistency, ever since; today it is one of the leading providers of such services in Europe.

Looking for a Challenge

Prior to starting up the company, both founders Steve and Tim were well-experienced in the field of telecommunications, having chalked up more than 25 years between them working for companies such as BT and GEC in Britain and America. In his time at BT, Steve had created BT Conferencing, set up a joint venture called Quip! and had later moved on to join the Caudwell group where he was also led the setting up of a fixed-line business called Reach Telecoms. Tim, meanwhile, helped to run a number of small GEC Telecom companies and had moved, in the early nineties to PictureTel Corporation, then a small company, and one of the pioneers in video conferencing - it was here, in fact, that that he had met Steve when the two men had been involved in a business deal.

Late in 2001, Tim and Steve were both 'looking for new challenges' at a time when 'nobody' was investing anything in startup companies following the collapse of the dotcom bubble. A few weeks after the September 11th tragedy, during a conversation in a coffee shop in London, they decided to channel their existing skills into creating a new company to provide new services to allow people to collaborate without being in the same location. At a time when most people were expecting the growth in collaboration services to come from video conferencing, Tim and Steve had come up with what they thought was a lucrative opportunity mainly in simple voice conferences coupled with web collaboration tools. They spotted that new technology was enabling much better services, and that there was a problem with the existing providers which a new company could solve.

Although BT had just about cornered the UK market at the time, the ways in which the service was executed by companies generally were, in Tim and Steve's eyes, outdated and slow. As Steve recalls, in order to set up a conference account the customer would have to call up the company and request it – the company would then set up an account, take your bank account details and, some considerable time later, get back to you with an access code that would enable you and your colleagues to join the call. It was a lengthy process every time you wanted to make a conference call, requiring call booking in advance with their provider.

'The established companies offering these services were hampered by expensive and old technology.'

The established companies offering these services were hampered by expensive and old technology which required large numbers of people to operate. Steve and Tim could see a very clear business opportunity: using the internet, they could set up a service that offered a considerably better service for customers, and at considerably lower cost to their new company, than the older systems used by the established competitors. The shocking terrorist attacks on the Twin Towers translated immediately into an increased demand for alternatives to business travel, boosting early demand for conference call and collaboration services.

Improving a Service

Armed with this idea, Tim and Steve realised that one of the key things that their business could provide was a real time 'transparent' kind of bill. They spoke to some of the big customers and industry analysts that they had known from previous ventures, and found that there was widespread dissatisfaction with the existing billing systems - which conference call customers felt all too often amounted to a 'messy pile of paper' with little traceability. Tim and Steve decided, therefore, to improve the billing system so that details such as who called, how long the call lasted and how much it cost were available through their online account immediately after the call.

They also wanted to market their service as a lower cost alternative than their competitors, whilst providing superior service levels. As a result, they decided on a price point below the average which was at that time dominated by giants such as BT – who had a list price of 22p per minute. Tim and Steve decided 12p a minute was a suitable price distinction without falling too low.

Then the two founders focussed on providing a better service. According to Steve and Tim, good service was the main advantage of MeetingZone – overall, conference call customers were not unhappy paying the current prices, but they were unhappy with the service they were getting. The founders' solution was to offer customers a unique self service model via the web where anyone could set up an account 'within a couple of clicks'; and their system didn't need customers to book a specific call

View of the Oxford offices.

time at all, but instead let them make conference calls whenever they wanted simply by dialling in with the appropriate account code. As conference calls were business affairs that often took place in environments where time was of essence, this idea made absolute sense to them; all they needed now was enough money to build the system and start selling it.

'£2 million was a lot of money for a raw startup.'

Tim and Steve spent several weeks building forecasts and drafting their business plan, which they needed to help them raise £2 million. Given the risk averse investment climate in 2002 they designed the plan to appeal primarily to those investors interested in a low-risk, short-term investment run by individuals who were experienced and knew the market. It included carefully planned milestones and both founders ensured that 'everyone knew there were lots of checks and balances' to ensure the growth of the business was going according to plan. As well as this, when presenting the business plan to investors they ensured that they referenced the good management team they had assembled and recruited, for example, the ex CEO of PictureTel Corporation as a board member. This reduced the apparent risk-factor a little further and encouraged investors to part with their money.

A sum of £2 million was a lot of money for a raw startup in the climate of 2002. In order to offer an 'impressive corporate service' from day one, Tim and Steve needed enough money to build really good software, as well as to fund a corporate class customer service team and professional marketing. It was their intention from the outset to get it right first time and go through only one funding round from which they hoped to get to profitability right away, which is almost unheard of for a start up businesses like this.

However, after approaching various Venture Capitalists in early 2002, the founders learned that most of them considered it an 'excessive' figure to attempt to raise – so they lowered their sights to raise the slightly smaller sum of £1.6 million which they calculated was the absolute minimum required. Tim and Steve spent months meeting various venture capitalists and other investors such as high net worth individuals, also known as business angels. This ultimately proved worth their while – they ended up raising £2.1 million! As soon as one Venture Capitalist (Springboard plc) had agreed to invest, they found it much easier to get other investors on board.

Once they had the funds, Tim and Steve began designing and building the service delivery platform and investing in the hardware and software. The first investment being the billing system – which cost them several hundred thousand pounds of license fees plus extra costs. Although this was expensive, Tim reveals that most of the deals they struck were on fantastic terms given the collapse of the Telecoms markets in 2002, one of the advantages of starting a business in a major downturn. The rest of the money, Tim says, went on funding the design team of software programmers that were working in offices he and Steve had borrowed in Milton Keynes over the summer of 2002.

'Do as much networking as possible so that you get to know a lot of people.'

They then turned to the issue of marketing. Having had much experience in larger businesses, they knew that their best route was simply to spread the word of their

Team photo, Christmas 2002.

new web-based business to existing contacts and previous major clients. It is a path that both men recommend to anyone starting up their own business; firstly, do as much networking as possible so that you get to 'know a lot of people', and then to work hard to make the most of this network; it's amazing, they say, 'how important your network is'. As well as this, they also spent a fair proportion of the initial funds hiring a PR agency in the hope of 'punching above our weight'. This proved very sensible, freeing up Steve and Tim to cultivate new clients, while their PR agency could work on spreading the story to potential newprospects. Tim explains that they decided to use Six Degrees, a PR agency that Tim's previous company, PictureTel, had used very successfully to launch their European market entry ten years earlier. As they specialised in providing business-to-business media relations, they were ideal for getting the word out into the wider market.

Envisaged Success

The company was launched in September 2002 after the company moved into rented offices on the Oxford Business Park, and secured the business of a major FTSE company within the first few weeks. Business started to grow very rapidly as clients appreciated the new approach from MeetingZone and word spread on its unique service offer.

Shortly after this Tim and Steve began to experiment with online marketing, using Google, which would become a significant new marketing approach. As well as this, they confess that they were fortunate in that during the first six months the PR activities paid off with 'considerable' press coverage in the business media and as a result business grew at a strong rate.

The company also started to see a second benefit from its investors – contacts. Their investors had an obvious incentive to see MeetingZone succeed, and some of them provided a number of contacts which led to new sales accounts. By delivering a substantially better product for customers than its competitors, MeetingZone also grew by word of mouth, as delighted customers talked to colleagues about the new company.

Their business had high initial overheads, but the nature of their technology-based approach meant that they could scale the business without a corresponding increase in overheads. Their revenues started rising between 5% and 10% every month, with a static cost base and after about two years they broke through into profitability, without needing to raise any more money from investors in line with their original business plan.

> '**MeetingZone would have run out of cash very quickly had the sales not appeared as predicted.**'

Despite what may appear to be an easy success, Tim says that trying to minimise cash drain whilst retaining a high level of service was their 'biggest challenge' at this time. He adds that it was in fact always something of a 'balancing act' to ensure that money invested in sales and customer support returned funds achieved a rapid payback. 'MeetingZone would have run out of cash very quickly had the sales not appeared as predicted` Tim revealed.

Finances are always a problem for young companies, and the founders also recall running into another cash-related problem when one of their key US suppliers was acquired by another company and attempted to renege on the original supply contract due to the highly favorable terms they had initially negotiated. As Tim reflects, although MeetingZone were ultimately successful in enforcing the contract with the supplier, it took a lot of stress, time and a lot of money. Anyone starting a new business should always be aware of the possibility of such issues.

Despite this, Tim and Steve are justifiably proud that, two years after the launch, when they had reached profitability and seen through a legal dispute, they had £300,000 left in the bank from the £2.1 million that had been invested.

Since such early figures, turnover has increased at an astounding rate, the first year's £75,000 growing to £4 million by the end of 2006. MeetingZone has also

Training the newly recruited team in Oxford, August 2002.

continued to innovate in all areas of its service offering keeping it well ahead of the competition and today has thousands of major corporations as clients and a complete suite of collaboration applications.

Such success, they say, is largely down to service innovation quality of their employees and the strength of the corporate class service provided. 'If we can't automate it we don't do it' claims Steve, 'the strength of the MeetingZone model is in the relentless application of new technology to keep overheads down and service levels high'.

From their previous jobs, Steve and Tim were both familiar with the process of early startups in the business world and also with the telecoms market they entered. Both men stress that this is key to the success of your business and they warn that if you are planning to start up a business you should always 'know your industry backwards'.

WHERE ARE THEY NOW?

Retaining a 40% share of the company, both Tim Duffy and Steve Gandy are still heavily involved with MeetingZone, which at last count had a market share of 5%-10% in the UK. Trying to build, in their own words, 'for the long-term rather than a quick win or exit' their focus is on continuing to build the brand, ultimately aiming to replicate the model outside the UK. They have recently completed several acquisitions which they have absorbed seamlessly into MeetingZone. With the world starting to focus on minimizing the impact of global business on the environment they are confident that a company at the leading edge of reducing business travel will continue to grow, which should be good for MeetingZone.

dyson

Dyson

Designing
from Dust

Company:	**Dyson Ltd**
Founders:	**James Dyson**
Age at start:	**45**
Background:	**Designer and inventor**
Start year:	**1992**
Business:	**Vacuum cleaner manufacture**

Today, Dyson is very much a household name; it advertises its revolutionary products prominently on television, they are on sale throughout the world, and its every move is written up in the national press. Yet a mere 15 years ago, you literally couldn't buy a Dyson vacuum cleaner anywhere in Britain. James Dyson prefers to think of himself as a designer rather than an entrepreneur; in fact, he excels at both. The business he founded currently exports to over 40 countries, and has achieved sales of more than £3 billion worldwide. Yet it all started with one man and an idea.

To accomplish this, James endured 20 years of debt, faced multiple lawsuits and learnt countless lessons on the temperamental nature of vacuum cleaner licensing agreements.

Innovative Pedigree

James Dyson is an engineer and designer. While studying at the Royal College of Art, James developed his dream: to be a modern day Brunel and to revolutionise the way products are designed. James' first product, his graduation piece, was the Sea Truck, which he designed for British inventor and entrepreneur Jeremy Fry in 1969. The Sea Truck was sold in more than 50 countries and has achieved sales of over $500 million to date. Jeremy gave James his first job, at Rotork Engineering, after he graduated and James was promoted to director only three years later. In this position, James discovered the difficulty of selling the commercially unfinished Sea Truck and learnt the importance of perfecting a design before its production.

In 1974 James chose to pursue inventing for himself, and left Rotork to design the award winning Ballbarrow, a deviation from the wheelbarrow, using a pneumatic balloon in place of the usual wheel. James believed he could modernise the traditional barrow, and so he left a highly paid, prestigious job. Throughout his career James has been driven by a desire to make technology work better.

He needed capital to fund his first venture, and persuaded two wealthy people he knew (one who was his brother-in-law) to invest, and Kirk-Dyson was founded. By March 1974 they had a prototype but six months into production the manufacturer they had chosen began raising its prices, leading to a decision to borrow another £45,000 to buy machinery from America and manufacture it themselves.

The Ballbarrow designed by James in 1974.

Here, James had his first taste of selling consumer goods. A journalist from *The Sunday Times* picked up on the invention: James notes the power that a 'tried and tested' article can have on sales, proving a product's worth. Soon, they were selling 45,000 Ballbarrows and turning over £600,000 a year. The company tried to export its products to America to grow sales, but ended up in a costly lawsuit with an American business which had produced a very similar product after taking on one of James' staff.

Cleaning Conundrum

During this time, James was renovating his house in the Cotswolds and was amazed at the inefficiency of his vacuum cleaner. Surprisingly, there seemed to be no obvious improvement if he used a new bag. Even investing in the most advanced model on the market, it clogged after use in just a few rooms, losing its suction. At Ballbarrow's factory, he was experiencing similar problems on a much larger scale: the industrial cleaner was also clogging up with dust during production. James found out that cyclones were often used for large-scale industrial cleaning, and was quoted £75,000 to install one.

'*He ripped the bag off his vacuum cleaner and rigged up a rudimentary cardboard cyclone with cereal packets and masking tape.*'

Instead of paying this colossal sum, James was inspired by a 30ft cyclone at a nearby sawmill that spun dust out of the air by a centrifugal force. After putting this technology to the test at the factory, James realised the potential of a miniature version of this to solve his domestic problem. He ripped the bag off his vacuum cleaner and 'rigged up a rudimentary cardboard cyclone' with cereal packets and masking tape. This foetal prototype essentially worked and drove James to seriously consider the potential of this creation.

Taking this idea first to the Kirk-Dyson board, presenting an opportunity to diversify from the limited gardening market into domestic appliances, James was met with pessimism. Not long after, financial friction eventually led to James being ousted from Kirk-Dyson by the other shareholders. As Ballbarrow's patent was owned by the company, not the designer, James left without his design – a mistake he vowed never to repeat.

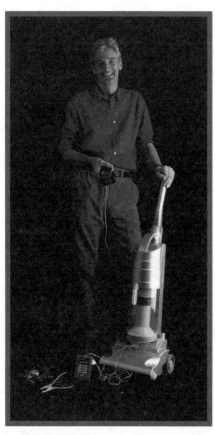

James with the DC01.

Alone again, James had to rely on his unswerving belief in his theoretical product; there was nothing to prove a cyclonic vacuum cleaner would work yet, and no evidence to persuade investors. Still, he set about designing one, through the gruelling process of trial and error. Shunned by his business partners and in need of financial backing, James approached an old friend with his prospective invention. Jeremy Fry provided £25,000, which James doubled by borrowing against his home. So James set up the Air Power Vacuum Cleaner Company, and began experimenting in an old, draughty coach house next to his home.

For five long years, he toiled over the design, attempting to develop his idea and win investment to construct his product. In 1983, after making more than 5,000 prototypes, he came up with a design which worked perfectly. Unlike most vacuum cleaners, which used a bag to store any dirt they collected, James' design used two cyclones to separate the dust from the air to stop the machine from clogging.

James explains that he was sure he had a mass-market design. Originally, James had intended the Air Power Vacuum Cleaner Company to manufacture the products itself, yet due to the lengthy and costly process, the company was deeply in debt and James was exhausted. Changing the company name to Prototypes Ltd, the business partners changed tack, now opting just to invent, and not manufacture. In the same year, the vacuum graced the cover of *Design Magazine*, festooned in bright pink plastic.

Sucking up the Courage

Having made its debut, James needed to find a manufacturer, ideally in Britain or Europe. James visited all the established manufacturers but surmised that although many companies understood his design, their main concern was to protect their

'They seemed more interested in maintaining the status quo – and of course, selling bags.'

own models: he was met with 'a staggering reluctance' to invest in new technology. Offering tools that would change the realm of cleaning forever, James recalls with understandable frustration that 'they seemed more interested in maintaining the status quo – and of course, selling bags': the vacuum bag market was valued at £100 million a year in the UK alone in 1984.

Although a few manufacturers did eventually offer to license his design, knowing the significance of his technology, James was unwilling to accept the 'paltry percentages' they offered, despite being in dire financial need of the customary payment he would have got when a deal was signed. It would have been easy to sell his technology in a one off payment but after the Ballbarrow experience, he was adamant that this time he would retain ownership. James also suspected that if he succumbed, his design would get swept under the carpet and never be made.

Jeremy Fry's Rotork came to his aid for a brief spell in 1983 and manufactured a few hundred vacuum cleaners. Although this was a long way off the mass-production James envisaged, significantly, the first ever models were manufactured and sold.

Meanwhile, James was still working hard trying to secure deals, always being disappointed when they fell through, mostly due to licensing disagreements. Aware that business culture in America was much more conducive to new technology, he started targeting the American market. Yet again, deals fell through with Black & Decker and Conair, both at the last minute. A deal was signed with Amway in April 1984, a cause for celebration, but within a matter of months it withdrew from the contract, accusing Prototypes Ltd of deceiving it as the product was not yet ready. A legal battle ensued lasting eight months, denying James the opportunity to re-license his product elsewhere until early 1985. He settled quickly due to legal costs and had to give back everything Amway had paid him, but eventually was free.

After these demoralising years, James was desperate to manufacture the cleaner himself, but financing this while the company was so heavily in debt was impossible: his only hope was to succeed in licensing his technology to one country to generate an income which he could use to fund his own manufacturing.

Eventually, in 1985, James stumbled upon a Japanese manufacturer offering him a reasonable deal. He sold the rights to the technology in Japan and at last began manufacturing vacuum cleaners. The machine, named 'G-Force', went on to win the 1991 International Design Fair prize in Japan and so impressed were Japanese consumers with the model that it became a status symbol and sold for $2,000 a pop.

Dyson's head office at Malmesbury.

With a retail product on the shelves, albeit not in the UK, James hired a small team of graduates from the Royal College of Art to develop the product in his coach house-turned-workshop; James imagined it would be easier to sell a ready-made product in America. However in 1987, as he was just about to sign a deal with Canadian company Iona to manufacture a carpet-cleaning version of the design, he discovered that Amway, the manufacturing juggernaut that had pulled out on a deal three years earlier, had begun producing vacuums with the cyclone design. James began what turned into a five-year legal battle, which meant that he had to spend all his royalties from the Japanese company on legal fees. More successfully, he also secured an agreement to sell his technology in the commercial market, and Johnson Wax launched an industrial cleaner.

By early 1990, the royalties from Japanese and finally American sales placated the company's bank manager and made the prospect of manufacturing in Britain vaguely feasible once more. The lawsuit with Amway had been settled, relieving funds but not enough to go into business alone.

James approached potential investors, but was categorically turned down because of the 'whimsical' idea of a designer running a business. What would *Dragons' Den* have made of him? Multiple applications for a bank loan were also dismissed, until eventually a sympathetic bank manager wangled James a £600,000 loan, guaranteed by a mortgage on his homes in London and Bath.

Product Perfection

In 1992, James recruited design engineers from the RCA to work on what he called the Dual Cyclone™ design, which was to be, for the first time, manufactured in his own name. Determined to perfect the design before its release, the team took their time, even though competitors were copying some of their unpatented design elements. In the long run, James believes, this paid off, and the perfectionist designer released an unrushed, finished version.

The first DC01 was completed on May 2 1992, James' 45th birthday. Its fundamental design, not only the technology, differentiated from other vacuum cleaners: early market research had suggested the consumer did not want a clear bin, yet now, it is one of the make's most popular features and competitors are copying it. James sold it from a practical perspective – you could see the machine working, and knew when it needed to be emptied.

To be able to manufacture, still more money was needed, so James decided to sell all the rights to his technology to the manufacturer in Japan. This generated nearly all of the £900,000 he needed to go into production: Dyson Ltd was born.

As production began, Dyson Ltd's first sale was made in July 1992 to Great Universal Stores, the largest mail order group in Britain. James recalls that after six hours of negotiations, he finally admitted to its chief buyer that he found its catalogue boring and felt it needed an injection of new technology, in the form of his Dyson DC01 cleaner. He reminisces that this candid approach 'finally sealed the deal – he took a thousand.' From this success, the company secured contracts with catalogues such as Littlewoods; initially he was cautious not to approach the high street retailers in case competitors got wind of the impending launch, James scrapped this strategy when John Lewis asked to take 250 DC01s.

As James and his team concentrated on selling, small, independent Italian tooling companies were contracted to make the gargantuan moulds needed in production and by the end of November 1992, the tools were transported to Wales, where Phillips Plastics was to produce the machines. Efficient workmanship meant the first DC01s came off the production line in January 1993. In April, a big order from Rumbelows set Dyson up with a solid base of orders: the future looked rosy.

However, on the rocky path to success, the manufacturer, Phillips, vastly raised its prices, forcing Dyson to gradually move production elsewhere. As happened so often in this story, a lawsuit ensued and forced Dyson to stop manufacturing for one crucial month. Yet again refusing to be defeated, James and his team quickly set up a production factory in an old Royal Mail warehouse and produced the very first DC01 exclusively made by a Dyson Ltd employee, in July 1993.

The Dyson Root 6™, the handheld cleaner that doesn't lose suction.

Fifteen years after his sawmill epiphany, James finally had his own business manufacturing his revolutionary cleaner. He had spent the staggering sums of £1.5 million on patents and £2-3 million on development.

> 'He had spent the staggering sums of £1.5 million on patents and £2-3 million on development.'

James believes that in the UK there is a tendency to over-value marketing, when 'having well-engineered products does the work for you – it speaks for itself'. With an unassailable design, and manufacturing in place, surely Dyson could sit back and watch consumers consume. Yet they were wary of buying an unknown brand, and shops promoted traditional models. Still, word spread as the 'intrinsic excellence of the machine' spoke for itself, receiving much acclaim through editorial coverage without a rigid advertising campaign. In under a year, Dyson Ltd turned over £2.4 million and after one year of retail, this had risen considerably to £9 million.

Through the first few years of retail, sales grew healthily, but only really took off when superstores Comet and Currys started to sell the DC01, which they did in 1995. Almost immediately, the DC01 became the best-selling vacuum cleaner in the UK, where it has stayed ever since.

On the verge of bankruptcy many times and frequently in the face of great adversity, James' unswerving belief in his groundbreaking technology prevailed. He explains that 'engineering and design are the driving forces behind everything I do'.

WHERE ARE THEY NOW?

James Dyson is still the sole owner of Dyson Ltd, which in 2005 made a profit of around £100 million.

Dyson Ltd continues to innovate and offer consumers new alternatives to old appliances, like the recently launched Dyson Digital Motor and its innovative hand dryer, Dyson Airblade. In 2000, it launched the Contrarotator washing machine and in 2003, took the American vacuum cleaner market by storm, exceeding targets by over 180%. Predictably, countless patent court cases ensued, including a battle with Hoover, from which Dyson emerged victorious.

THE BLACK FARMER™

The Black Farmer

How to Meat Consumer Demands

Company:	**The Black Farmer**
Founders:	**Wilfred Emmanuel Jones**
Age at start:	**47**
Background:	**Trained at the BBC, then founded a marketing company**
Start year:	**2004**
Business:	**Specialist sausage and sauces producer**

From the early days of tending to his father's allotment in Birmingham, Wilfred Emmanuel Jones knew that it was his dream to escape the 'urban jungle' of the city and own his own farm. But it was not until nearly 40 years later that his dream became a reality and the idea behind his home-grown brand, The Black Farmer, began to take shape. After two years of struggle to convince major supermarkets to stock his rage of sausages and sauces at the prices which he demanded, The Black Farmer is now enjoying placement virtually across the board, including, at last, in that greatest of supermarket giants, Tesco.

Love of the Land

When he was a young boy, Wilfred moved with his family from Jamaica to Birmingham, taking him from the rural home he had known to a very different life in the heart of a large city. In Birmingham, his father gave him responsibility for running a nearby allotment, which he loved so much that he began to dream about one day running his own farm. This love of agriculture has stayed with him ever since, throughout career stints in both catering and television.

Wilfred's determination and persistence are evident from the tale of how he got his first job in TV. Initially he deluged the BBC with phone calls and letters, eventually getting a job as a researcher for a food and drinks programme. He then worked his way up the career ladder by means of the BBC's graduate trainee scheme, and after years of promotion after promotion, eventually reached a producing/directing role that he was able to carry on as a freelancer.

Although Wilfred admits that working for the BBC constituted a 'good, glamorous life' he also says there was no real money in it, and that he realised he was always going to stay as a producing director, which wasn't enough to satisfy his ambition. As a result, in 1993 Wilfred began the process of moving away from television. After

Wilfred's farm on the Devon Hills, bordering Cornwall.

three years of working in TV part-time on a freelance basis, he was finally able to move fully away.

Wilfred really wanted to buy a farm, and decided to set up his own food and drinks marketing company which he hoped would provide him with the money he would need. He chose food, he says, as he felt this was his 'skill-base,' since both of his jobs thus far had involved produce. And since his time at the BBC had taught him how to deal with people and the media, it was, he says, something of a natural move to try to promote food products.

Before setting up his marketing business, Wilfred had calculated his costs and realised he had enough savings to be able to afford the mortgage on his house for three months. As a result, he gave himself those three months in which to gain some business – after which time, if he had failed, he said he would return to his old profession. He set up quickly, and soon won projects to raise the public profiles of (then much smaller) brands such as Cobra Beer, KETTLE Chips and Loyd Grossman, using a mix of advertising and PR.

A Banger of an Idea

This business in fact brought in so much money that in 1999, aged 42, Wilfred could afford to buy a farm – much like that he had envisaged aged 11. He carried on running his marketing company at this point, and was successful enough that he did not have to earn his living from farming. Wilfred hired someone to run the farm for him and has since remained what he calls a 'gentleman farmer,' rather than a hands-on one.

'He wanted to buy a decent sausage for one of his favourite meals, the English breakfast.'

Wilfred happens to love sausages. He had increasingly felt that the sausage market had become lazy, dominated by the supermarkets' own premium ranges. He wanted to buy a decent sausage for one of his favourite meals, the English breakfast. Unable to find it in supermarkets, Wilfred became passionate about offering the public an alternative which met his own high standards at an affordable price.

The marketing skills Wilfred had been using for other people's products proved invaluable when it came to launching his own brand. Since buying his farm, Wilfred recalls how he was struck, on numerous occasions, by the absence of black faces

The Black Farmer's Premium Pork Sausages.

in the countryside. This was reinforced by his neighbour referring to him as 'the black farmer', and inspired him to come up with The Black Farmer brand. It made sense to use a name strongly associated with himself, and which he says was 'strong, bold and upfront, as well as being positive about my colour. The name also forces people to think more about issues of race and stereotype and in particular, farming and diversity.'

Wilfred has understandably continued to take an interest in the theme of farming and diversity. He bought an advertisement in a March 2005 edition *The Sunday Times*, encouraging young black people to come and compete for scholarships on his farm; Channel 4 filmed the programme, and broadcast it later that year.

Taste Testing at County Fairs

Wilfred's first task was to find a manufacturer who could make the sausages to his requirements. Wilfred did not want to produce the meat on his own farm, he says, as having worked with a lot of brands through his marketing company, he realised that trying to do the manufacturing yourself is what often caused a lot of companies problems. Luckily, he found a local company that was able to make the sausages for him, sourcing the meat from other local farms.

'You can have the best packaging in the world but people need to try the product.'

One thing that marketing had taught Wilfred was the importance of very good dialogue with your customers. So although it was always his intention to sell The Black Farmer produce to supermarkets and ultimately to grow The Black Farmer into a well-known international brand, he decided initially to sell on a much smaller scale and in an environment where he could talk to the customers – county fairs. Wilfred wanted to get people to try his sausages and give him feedback. Not only would this assist him when it came to trying to sell the product to the buyers in major stores, but

Wilfred and a willing taste tester.

also in building customer loyalty. As Wilfred warns, 'you can have the best packaging in the world but people need to try the product'.

But before selling any sausages, Wilfred did have to design his packaging. He decided to use a photograph of himself in silhouette as his logo, since he had seen that brands based on people could suffer abroad if consumers did not recognise the person, and he wanted his brand to grow internationally in the future. This way, he says, people could place their own emotional attachments there. He also suggests that part of the reason for the striking image, which contains a highly contrasted image of black and orange, was that he wanted the brand was to be controversial and 'in your face'.

Wilfred began taking his product to county fairs across the country. He spent 'a fortune' – approximately £250,000 – marketing his sausages, as well as a small selection of sauces he had commissioned from local producers, before selling to any supermarkets. Most of this money went on allowing people to sample the sausages, which Wilfred wanted to do in order to develop a strong and loyal customer base. Cleverly, he has tried to leverage his customers' support by getting them to sign a 'petition' on his website asking for The Black Farmer sausages to be made more widely available in supermarkets.

Wilfred also got valuable market research by talking to customers. For example, he found out which recipes were most popular, which later helped him choose which three of his range of six sausages he should try to push into supermarkets.

During those early weeks of touring county fairs, Wilfred also spent time approaching supermarkets, trying to set up a meeting with their buyers. Unsurprisingly, the supermarkets did not respond instantly, so while waiting to hear from them, Wilfred began videoing some of the customers who approached The Black Farmer stall at county fairs, so he could show the supermarket buyers just how well consumers reacted to his products.

His resilience paid off. After a period of about eight months selling at county fairs and to the odd farm shop and delicatessen, Wilfred started to get meetings with buyers at supermarkets such as Asda, Tesco, Waitrose and Budgens. His sales pitch consisted largely of showing the videos he had made from county fairs, as well as providing information about the sausages, which were the only The Black Farmer product to be aimed specifically at the supermarkets. Although none of these meetings ended in immediate success, Wilfred continued to 'badger' supermarkets – as he had done with the BBC nearly 30 years earlier – and was ultimately rewarded for his efforts.

Nine months after his first meeting with Asda, they agreed to try a small range of his products. He jokes that this was done mainly as a means of keeping him quiet! The fact that Asda were the first supermarket to stock The Black Farmer sausages was, he confesses, something of a shock. He had originally thought that the idea of his 'affordable premium' sausages would appeal most to Waitrose, as their business ethic seemed most reflective of his brand values. In fact, he found that Waitrose were 'pretty slow on the uptake'. Other supermarkets signed up at a rate of around one every few months after Asda, speeding up as he was able to demonstrate that his sausages were selling well at more and more supermarkets. Waitrose were in fact the last supermarket to stock The Black Farmer products, not doing so until September 2006.

Since then, business has been booming. One of the youngest businesses in this book, The Black Farmer is understandably smaller; its turnover for the first year was £500,000, and in 2006 was £1.3 million. His produce is now stocked in seven supermarkets nationwide and is considered to be one of the UK's fastest growing brands, showing just how far you can get with persistence and determination.

WHERE ARE THEY NOW?

Wilfred Emmanuel Jones is heavily involved in The Black Farmer today. He continues to sell and promote the product range at county fairs across the country as well as sell to supermarkets.

The brand has successfully added some other meat products such as bacon, ham and chicken, and Wilfred hopes to ultimately launch a sister brand entitled The Black Farmer's Wife which will sell related farm produce such as cheeses and yoghurt. In the meantime, he is continuing to use his growing profile to educate the world about the importance of local produce and the fallibility of supermarkets.

The Fabulous Bakin' Boys

A Rising Success

Company:	The Fabulous Bakin' Boys
Founders:	**Gary Frank**
Age at start:	**38**
Background:	**Stock market trader then unemployed**
Start year:	**1997**
Business:	**Baked foods manufacturer and retailer**

Finding Your Calling

Some might say the **Fabulous Bakin' Boys** was a product of divine intervention. Its founder, Gary Frank, went into the bakery business after receiving a message that was 'hard to ignore'. Not a religious man, he was more surprised than anyone when he was visited in a dream by 'an old boy' in a long white gown, with a long white beard, and long white hair, 'like something out of a 1950s Cecil B. DeMille production of The Bible'. And what did this old boy have to say for himself? He said 'Gary, go and make doughnuts'. So he did. Gary opened the Delicious Donut Company in 1989, making, selling and delivering doughnuts himself to local shops and delis in Oxford and London. Eighteen years later, his company, which was re-launched as the Fabulous Bakin' Boys in October 1997, is raking in £12 million a year and his range of cakes, muffins and flapjacks graces bakery fixtures in all the major supermarkets.

Gary moved to New York in 1982, after graduating from Oxford with a degree in Philosophy and Psychology, and started trading futures on the stock market. He lost all his money, along with many others, following a major market crash in 1987, and subsequently came back to England with his tail between his legs. The night 'the dream' took place, Gary had been back living in England for nine months. Unemployed and living on the dole in Oxford, it's fair to say he wasn't exactly in the ideal position to start making doughnuts.

Against All Odds

Never one to let such trivialities as having no money, no knowledge of business and even less knowledge of baking stop him, he started looking into the idea. Inspired by this rare prophetic moment and determined that making doughnuts was what he was put on this earth to do, Gary focused on the one thing that he did have going for him, plenty of free time. So, unfazed by the prospect of starting 'completely from square one', he started 'looking around', going into corner shops, delis, cafes and sandwich bars around Oxford. One thing soon became clear; they weren't actually selling the products that he had in mind, the kind of ring doughnuts that are 'everywhere' in New York.

Encouraged by this gap in the market, Gary began searching for people to help him produce and manufacture his product, and by a stroke of luck that was almost too coincidental, found exactly what he was looking for in a local, Aylesbury-based firm, the Doughnut Company of America (DCA). 'They were a company that made ingredients, mixes and machines, and everything I could possibly need to set up a doughnut company', he says. Keeping from them the fact he was on the dole, he sold to them his brilliant plan for selling American doughnuts in Britain.

Gary holding a tray of muffins a few years after the launch of FBB.

'He took to the streets of Oxford, asking owners of local shops if they would sell his doughnuts.'

After approaching DCA, Gary started working with them on recipes until they came up with a product he was happy with. So, armed with his samples, he took to the streets of Oxford, asking owners of local shops if they would sell these doughnuts if he continued to make them, and got the response he was looking for – they would.

A Prophecy Fulfilled

With a product ready to sell and potential customers waiting to buy, Gary realised he was going to need a proper business plan to get the funding he needed to get the venture off the ground. With no idea where to start he got in touch with his local Business Link and started learning the basics. Gary worked out he would need

£30,000 to get the business off the ground, and managed to raise £15,000 from friends and family who liked the sound of his idea.

Short of £15,000, he took his business plan to a bank, not expecting them to agree but thinking, 'there's no harm in asking'. However, in another stroke of luck, they, too, gave him the answer he was looking for, offering to lend Gary £15,000 despite him having no security to guarantee the loan. All he needed now was a small industrial unit between Oxford and London to be his base camp, which he managed to find in Witney. The unit measured 1,000sq ft and he managed to 'blag' most of his equipment from DCA, on the basis that he would buy all his mixes and ingredients from them.

All his early marketing effort was concentrated on the packaging for the products, for which Gary enlisted the help of a designer friend of his, who came up with a logo, graphics and pack designs, relatively cheaply. With a budget that didn't leave much for promotional activity, Gary knew he would be relying heavily on word of mouth for the business to grow.

Gary's last task was to buy a second-hand van he could use to deliver his doughnuts; then he was ready. When Gary had the dream he knew nothing about doughnuts, or business for that matter. Six months later, the Delicious Donut Company was founded on May 1, 1989.

Learning the Hard Way

The first year was a hard slog for Gary, who ended up working 20-hour days and taking care of almost everything himself to get the business up and running. 'I had one girl who used to come in and help me with the production but other than that I did everything myself, the manufacturing, the deliveries, the paperwork, the sales, making the tea and everything.' Gary and his assistant would start work at midnight, and spend four or five hours making the doughnuts. As she finished her shift, Gary would load up his van, delivering to corner shops and sandwich bars in London four days a week, and Oxford twice a week. He would then drive back to Witney, take care of the admin and paperwork, snatching a few hours sleep at around 8pm before starting all over again the next day.

'I did everything myself, the manufacturing, the deliveries, the paperwork, the sales, making the tea and everything.'

The Bakin' Boys' grumpy free logo.

It took some time for this hard work to pay off. 'The first year was crap' admits Gary, 'the one flaw in the plan was that nobody liked these flipping doughnuts. The old boy gave me a bum steer, he should have told me to go and make muffins.' He had spent two thirds of the initial £30,000 getting the business off the ground, leaving him £10,000 working capital for the first year. By the end of this year he had turned over about £45,000, but made a £15,000 loss.

However, by the end of this year, in another lucky coincidence, Gary started buying in some new products. He began selling muffins and flapjacks which he bought from Andrew and Sara Staples, a couple that ran a takeaway pizza business from the industrial unit next door to his in Witney. 'The muffins did sell, unlike the doughnuts, which didn't,' Gary explains. Suddenly the Delicious Donut Company was developing a range, and the sales of muffins in particular were going through the roof. As a result the company made a profit by the end of its second year, on a £250,000 turnover, and it's been profitable ever since. Selling the other products was the major turning point in the fortunes of the Delicious Donut Company, and, like many of the key events in this company's history, was born out of mere coincidence, says Gary. 'Sometimes in business things just happen, and they end up being quite significant.'

Diversifying the Range

Between 1989 and 1996, the business was growing at a fast pace. Gary's brother, Jon, came on board as a partner in the second year, along with a small sales team, and the business expanded steadily. Gary gradually extended the range and insists that the company, which was still largely a niche player in terms of the individually-wrapped products it was offering in the UK, 'drove the whole snack and bakery sector' for many years after the launch. They managed to tap into the catering sector, working with big contract caterers, such as Sodexho to get their cakes into school, factory and office canteens. From the beginning, 95% of the range was made in-house.

They had developed a range of single-serve individually wrapped muffins, cookies, cakes and flapjacks and came up with a brand to put on these wrappers called 'BakeHouse Cakes'. The company was turning over around £3 million but still hadn't cracked the supermarkets, which was the ultimate goal.

'We were called The Delicious Donut Company, but we didn't actually make doughnuts.'

Gary had stopped selling the doughnuts after his hard work in the first year of the business had resulted in poor sales, and he had realised that the market was for muffins, flapjacks and cookies. Armed with the lessons he had learned from his startup year, he decided that the company needed a change of image; a name, brand and identity that reflected what it had become. 'We were called The Delicious Doughnut Company, but we didn't actually make doughnuts,' he explains.

Gary decided that, if they were ever going to break into retail, they needed to take their enthusiasm into the market place and offer something different, fun and dynamic that was going to appeal to both the buyers at Tesco, and to their customers. He noticed that the bakery sections were filled with either own-label, private-label or Mr Kipling products, and 'Mr Kipling makes lovely cakes but they're not exactly the most dynamic and funky kind of brand. In fact, there weren't any dynamic, funky brands on the cake fixture,' says Gary. He felt that his own 'BakeHouse Cakes' brand was dull, twee and predictable, and decided it was time for a change.

Putting the Fun into Flapjacks

Gary describes his business as 'fun and irreverent'; a business that doesn't take itself too seriously. He wanted to create a brand which encapsulated this message, and offer the supermarkets a point of difference that would give them a reason to put his products on their shelves.

It was the thinking that the company had outgrown its original image that drove the re-launch in 1997. But Gary couldn't find many people who shared this view. After seeking advice from lots of people in the trade and from design agencies, the overwhelming response was one of 'if it ain't broke, why fix it?' Gary was being constantly reminded that he had a business that was doing very well, in a very nice niche, and besides, 'Mr Kipling had a marketing budget that was bigger than my turnover'.

'I find nothing more motivational than people telling me I can't do something.'

However, this only succeeded in strengthening his determination, 'it wasn't exactly big encouragement, but I find nothing more motivational than people telling me I can't do something,' he says.

Gary eventually appointed a design consultancy based in Cheltenham, to take on the task, giving them a blank canvas on which to create a brand that reflected what 'the boys' (the two brothers) were all about. And so, after a soul searching five month process in which the consultancy and Gary worked to encapsulate the very essence of the business, The Fabulous Bakin' Boys was launched on October 1 1997, with a brand new logo and one succinct statement with which to define their new brand: 'unsuitable for grumpy people'.

The company won its first contract with Sainsbury's in 1998. They made a smooth transition into the mainstream and are now regulars on the shelves of all the major multiples.

Gary surrounded by packaged Bakin' Boys products.

WHERE ARE THEY NOW?

At age 48, Gary Frank is still behind the wheel as the company's managing director, or 'head boy', leading the company alongside his brother Jon, who is commercial director, or 'big chief muffin'. The Fabulous Bakin' Boys is no longer a niche player, and Gary has had to contend with some of the 'bigger boys' gunning for his business, including stiff competition from Mr Kipling and McVities who now offer a similar product range. But never short of determination, Gary has risen to the challenge, and has carried on growing through it. 'We've had to deal with it, and we have done', he explains.

The boys have expanded into a 80,000 sq ft factory in Witney, and currently have 150 staff. Gary is now married with three children, but believes it was helpful that he was young, free and single when he started up the business. But even after running a gruelling 24/7 operation for all that time, Gary is still certain about one thing – running a company is much easier than running after three boys!

The Sage Group plc

At the Forefront of Technology

Company:	**Sage**
Founders:	**David Goldman and Dr Paul Muller**
Age at start:	**Goldman 44**
Background:	**Entrepreneur, rocket scientist**
Start year:	**1981**
Business:	**Business management software**

Sage is by some way the largest of the businesses featured in this book, and is one of the greatest startups in Britain in the last 30 years. It is one of the world's leading suppliers of accounting software for businesses, but also now provides a wide range of business software and related services. Its turnover for 2006 was over £930 million, on which it made over £240 million in profit; it is one of Britain's top 100 companies, valued at more than £3 billion. Yet it, too, began as an idea that a small group of normal people had one day.

'Sometimes it is the little things a business does that that can create a new market.'

Often lost amongst the big ideas and flamboyant personalities of successful entrepreneurship is the fact that sometimes it is the little things a business does, the small innovations, that that can create a new market and change the way a new breed of entrepreneurs run their businesses.

Solving a Problem

In 1981 Newcastle entrepreneur David Goldman had a not untypical business problem. He had been in the printing business for 20 years and one of the drawbacks for his company was the number of quotations he had to constantly give to prospective customers.

Meanwhile, Dr Paul Muller, a US citizen with the claim to fame of being one of the four key navigators of the first Apollo to land on the moon, was lecturing on Astronomy at Newcastle University. He was also an expert in the emerging world of computing. While in the city he set up a computer business and as chance would have it, he met with David.

At the University, Dr Muller was also involved with computing students who were exploring ways of streamlining business processes – and one of their projects was a bookkeeping package to assist a local accountancy firm. The team of students, which included Graham Wylie, who later joined the business and went on to become Technical Director and then Managing Director in the UK, wrote an accounting software programme which more accurately estimated the cost of company printing jobs, as well as managing their basic accounting.

When David sampled this software, the entrepreneur in him was stimulated: he recognised the opportunity to sell this specially crafted software to a wider market. And so it was that Sage was created – dedicated to selling the estimating programme,

Sage's former offices.

at first targeting other printing businesses. Sadly, David died in 1999, but current Chief Executive, Paul Walker, who joined the company as Financial Controller in 1984 when it had only seven employees on its payroll, remembers the fledgeling years. The name Sage, 'like so many of the founding features of the business' was born out of an idea which, as Paul remembers, 'started in the Rose and Crown pub opposite Tyne Tees television'. One of the team suggested the name and the identity developed from there.

Dr Muller as Technical Director championed the use of this innovative, new software language for bookkeeping which formed the backbone of the Sage product range for many years to come and on the back of this a truly world class product was created. Sage Sovereign, which later became known as Sage Line 50.

Customer Focus

David knew that the best way to sell their software was to show it to potential customers. Unlike most software companies at the time, who focussed on the technology of their programmes, Sage focussed on their customers, spelling out clearly what their product could do to make life easier for businesses. So David and Graham crisscrossed the country, visiting companies and demonstrating their product.

This method of selling the software proved effective, but was extremely time-consuming, and required long hours of traveling to market the product. They began to discuss alternative methods of getting the Sage products out there, and developed an approach which would later come to fruition.

The company began to recruit locally, bringing in mainly graduates to help manage demand, but also to design more software for what was becoming a very lucrative market.

Nigel Platt joined the company in 1984 aged 18, fresh out of sixth form, the fifth person on the company's payroll. He still works at Sage today and recalls the early years.

'It was a very small team and we all did a bit of everything', he said. 'Much of my job was making up discs for customers. There were not standardised operating platforms then so the discs we supplied were in all sorts of formats and sizes.'

'This proved to be a costly distraction and took us away from what the business was truly about.'

The ever-changing face of the software and computing market presented the next major challenge for the still youthful company. The success of the sector was obvious to all, yet Sage had to be careful not to diversify too soon. Paul explains, 'In the early days we got into an emerging market for simple network products which enables businesses to link PCs together, this included the production of a microprocessor and we invested in developing this and making it more powerful. This proved to be a costly distraction and took us away from what the business was truly about and our main area of expertise.'

Paul also remembers a time in 1985 when Sage's future was in no way stable, 'although our turnover almost doubled, in 1984-85 we made a sizeable loss and, like many companies, I had to beg the bank for an overdraft and ask when I could send cheques off. There seemed to be no question of receiving more venture capital so something had to change.'

Standing Out From the Growing Crowd

The change which kick-started Sage's success came at a time when David was working hard to develop Sage's branding. At an exhibition he attended in 1985, David experienced a moment of insight into the future when he saw a new kind of computer demonstrated.

Current Chief Executive Paul Walker, taken in the 1990s.

Former Managing Director Graham Wylie, also taken in the 90s.

'There seemed to be no possibility of receiving more venture capital so something had to change.'

'Alan Sugar brought out his Amstrad PCW 8526, the first real desktop PC. It was a curious item and utilised different sized discs but was affordable at around £350.' Paul recalls that 'we were selling our software then for several hundred pounds but we had to adjust our strategy, so we developed a package for the PCW at £99. We took it to numerous exhibitions and the cash just started rolling in.'

To aid this growth David and Graham, with a recently recruited Sales Director, began to build a network of resellers across the country in order to give their rapidly growing list of customers face-to-face support and advice for their Sage products. These sellers were themselves entrepreneurs wanting to break into the emerging business software market. Sage offered the resellers marketing materials and phone-based technical support and the network grew rapidly ensuring customers could get face to face support and advice for their Sage products. They encouraged the resellers to use the same customer-focused message about how their software would make running a business easier.

From this relatively novel approach to their expansion, the founders' view of the business changed from that of a new venture they were still thinking and deciding about in short-term increments to one that required a strategy with a longer view.

Another key driver for growth, and a differentiator to its competitors was Sage's technical support provided by phone. This was an early part of the offer, helping customers to learn how to use and get the most out of their software and it provides additional revenues through an annual service contract, as well as enhancing loyalty.

Sage's head office in North Park, Newcastle which they moved into in 2004.

The services Sage offers have continued to expand and today 65% of its revenues are from services such as support.

David led the business to flotation in 1989 at which point the business had 50 employees, a turnover of £9 million, profits of £2 million and a market capitalisation of £21 million. He initiated Sage's acquisitive strategy which started in 1988 with the acquisition of Sky Software, a mid-market provider, and following flotation numerous acquisitions followed in the US, Mainland Europe and emerging markets such as China, India and Malaysia.

David received an MBE for his services to the computer industry and in 1992 he was named Entrepreneur of the Year by *The Times* newspaper.

WHERE ARE THEY NOW?

In 1985 Dr Muller left to pursue other interests. He still speaks of two major undertakings in his life – navigating Apollo and being one of the original founders of Sage. By 1989, David Goldman had led the company to a position where it could be floated on the London Stock Exchange. Since then the company has expanded rapidly. David Goldman went on to become Chairman in 1994 and when he retired due to ill health in 1997 Michael Jackson, an early investor in Sage became the Chairman and Paul Walker, became Chief Executive. Michael and Paul continued to build on the company's international expansion and led the company into the FTSE 100, where it has remained. Sadly David Goldman died in 1999. Graham Wylie who had the role of Managing Director for the UK business retired from the business in 2003, to be succeeded by Paul Stobart.

Extreme Group

An Adventurous
Business

Company:	**Extreme Group**
Founders:	**Al Gosling**
Age at start:	**24**
Background:	**Originally founded a TV distribution company and an athlete management business**
Start year:	**1995**
Business:	**Extreme Group building and developing the Extreme brand**

Extreme is a vibrant collection of businesses themed around extreme sports, such as skateboarding, snowboarding and surfing, and the lifestyle that surrounds these sports. The original business was the Extreme Sports Channel, and all the other businesses have stemmed from this. The Extreme Group is hugely well known within its target audience group, and has become, excuse us, extremely successful, with turnover in excess of £22 million, and more than 250 staff in over 70 countries.

Self-taught Business Sense

Dynamic founder Al Gosling readily admits that academia was never his strong point, which he says partly prompted his move into the entrepreneurial field at the young age of 18, fresh from attaining two mediocre A-Levels. For a few years Al experimented with running every teenager's dream, a music management business. Then, aged 21, he set off for the Bahamas to combine an outdoor-lifestyle with what he refers to as his 'studying' – working as a pilot, dive master and yacht captain for a marine research company. It was during his time there that he decided that when he returned to the UK he wanted to set up a business which would take advantage of the skills he had cultivated in the extreme sports he was passionate about, such as windsurfing, kite-surfing and mountaineering.

'The concept was not to emulate what they were doing but to step sideways and do it another way.'

After a year and a half in the Bahamas, he returned in 1995 'bloody-minded' and determined to make good of his plans, bringing in a friend who had just graduated from university to help him set up not one, but two businesses. Setting his sights high, he admits that these two businesses were strongly inspired by the success of Mark McCormack, founder of International Management Group, in both Sports Management and TV-production, and says that 'the concept was not to emulate what they were doing but to step sideways and do it another way'. As a result, the plan was to raise the funds to set up firstly, an athlete management business, which made use of skills acquired during his time in music management, and secondly, a TV distribution company that worked with producers of shows which featured extreme sports.

Although Al admits to having doubts right from the beginning that the businesses would be successful, he talks of his passion for extreme sports as the drive behind setting the businesses up. Though he neither carried out any formal market research nor even wrote a business plan as such, he was convinced that a loyal community of adventure-seekers existed and felt sure, as entrepreneurs so often do, that there was a market out there longing to be reached.

Establishing Extreme

After moving back to his parents' house in the summer of that year, Al needed to raise money to fund his new businesses. He pitched to his parents and various friends, used his own savings, and managed to raise £18,000. He was now ready to start his business.

Al at the beach.

He contacted a friend who was working in TV distribution, and asked about various business issues to do with contracts for TV rights, which he knew little about. Al put himself through a crash-course in TV rights, gathering the rest through 'common sense' and by 'working it out'. His first business idea was to sign up the rights to TV programmes about different extreme sports from the programme makers, and then sell these rights onto countries around the world.

Now knowing roughly how the sector worked, Al then set about marketing the business, named Extreme International. At this stage, the self-confessed outdoor lifestyle fan was working 10 or 12 hours a day to try to get his business up and running. Initially spending the majority of the money on telephone calls and fax bills in a largely pre-internet era, he remembers that living and working at home did at least save on rent!

To find programmes he could sign up to distribute, Al attended several appropriate TV trade shows such as *MIP-TV* and *SportEL Miami*. Once he had a reasonable list of programmes signed up, his next task was to sell on the rights to TV companies around the world. Al found himself travelling all over the place trying to chase the producers in each country in order to sell them him his programmes. Although this was expensive and time consuming, the commitment paid off over the years and Al's

An Extreme snowboarder in action.

TV distribution business managed to run on a break-even basis, with every penny earned being re-invested.

A year into the venture, when things were going well for Extreme International, the friend who had helped Al set the company up decided to leave, and so Al bought him out. Al recalls this as one of his lowest points in the startup years.

At around the same time it was becoming clear that the athlete management company was being left behind, and slowly but surely Al decided to close it. With twenty athletes on the books, the business was taking up a greater amount of time than the rewards it was yielding. Having been very athlete management focused for the first five or so months the business had moved very quickly onto the TV side of things.

'It's not so much about picking yourself up,' he says now, 'as much as getting through it; if your business is strong, it will survive.'

In the four years following his 1995 launch, Al moved the company's headquarters from his parents' house to an office in London, and took on seven people to work at the growing business. As is common for this sector, there were a few close calls where, according to Al, 'we nearly went bust due to TV channels – our clients – not paying us and stretching payment terms'. Al dealt with these one at a time, focussing on each issue and finding a way through. 'It's not so much about picking yourself up,' he says now, 'as much as getting through it; if your business is strong, it will survive.' But by late 1999, his company had grown its turnover to £1.5 million.

'Proudly proclaiming itself to be the leading TV distribution business in the world selling extreme sports.'

Al could see clearly almost right away that the niche he had found was a strong one, as there were few other people in television distribution that focused on the initially small market of extreme sports. Al took advantage of his company's early lead, and worked hard to develop a reputation for his company as *the* specialist in that area, proudly proclaiming itself to be the 'leading TV distribution business in the world selling extreme sports'.

He could also see that interest in extreme sports was growing steadily. While many people thought that each individual extreme sport was little more than a fad – illustrated by an explosion of interest in skateboarding in the late 1970s which died a quick death – Al saw that many of the people who liked one sport also liked others, and that this growth in interest was increasing steadily and becoming part of youth culture in a bigger way; as a result, he believed that this would continue. What a difference a bit of faith and good timing so often makes in business.

Becoming Extremely Successful

Al can pinpoint the exact moment when he decided to transform Extreme International into the brand we know today. During a car journey in Suffolk, four and a half years after the company's launch, he recalls turning to one of his team and saying that the next stage for the company was a television channel. It was a natural move, since there was no TV station which catered specifically to the extreme sports sector, the

Extreme snowboarders.

world of television was changing significantly as digital TV was taking off, providing hundreds of TV channels to consumers for the first time, which led cable and satellite operators to seek new channels to serve to their customers. And Extreme's reputation as leading figures in the industry made them the obvious business to make this happen.

Two months later, the rest of the team were told and the process began, kick-started by talks with two visionary men, Stephen Cohen and Mark Schneider, who were running Europe's largest cable company UPC at the time. This eventually led to the establishment of the Extreme Sports channel and the setting up of a joint venture with the cable company. The cable company contributed what Al refers to as 'cash and infrastructure', while Al's team provided the programming and knowledge of the sector.

The new TV channel needed a new logo and so Al contacted one of his friends who ran a small design agency in Soho. Along with some of his more 'creative friends' Al began to develop what were to be the foundations of the Extreme brand. Although he says he did not at that time have the vision for the dramatic expansion that Extreme would later see, Al was very clear in wanting what he refers to as a 'stamp' that would work equally well at the top right-hand corner of a TV as it would on a variety of products and services which he hoped to develop business around and license out. Extreme Sports was an obvious name for the channel, clearly stating what it was about. Al and his team of friends then came up with the distinctive black and white oval-shape with an 'e' above an 'X'. This, they felt, had all the key aspects they were looking for – a strong image that is easily memorable and looks slightly rebellious, and one which fitted in with the style of thier target market. Al notes that the logo has endured very well, still working for its market today, which is unusual in what is traditionally a fast moving sector.

> '*As long as there are enough positives levelling out the negatives, rock and roll!*'

The Extreme Sports Channel launched in Holland in May 1999 and then on Sky in 2000. It proved to be a success almost from the word go, with many enquiries flooding in from the cable and satellite companies in the first week, and 10 countries signing up to the channel by the end of its first year. Though impressive, not everything went strictly according to plan. Al notes that he missed the opportunity to take a channel in America two years later; at the time he felt that he was too young and inexperienced and was holding out for a better deal. He now admits he should have taken the deal that was on the table.

Nevertheless, Al's outlook has been unwavering from the

BMX star Zach Shaw.

outset: that it is easy to be cheerful if the pros outweigh the cons; 'as long as there are enough positives levelling out the negatives, rock and roll!' It is this resilience to negativity that is at the heart of the Extreme brand and provides the foundation for the company's 'relaxed, live life to the max' approach. It has also helped Extreme grow. Before long Al brought in several angel investors who, attracted by the channel's success and growth potential, invested approximately £2.9 million in expansion cash for the business.

The company used some of this cash to launch a multitude of Extreme branded businesses covering drinks, hotels, an online shop, a clothing range, and even theme parks, all of which help spread the Extreme brand way way beyond the television channel.

WHERE ARE THEY NOW?

Al bought out his early investors in 2005 and remains very much hands on at what is now named the Extreme Group, overseeing all major decisions about the brand. The TV channel now broadcasts to 55 countries and in 12 languages, and as a group Extreme is active in 23 sectors and in more than 70 countries.

The group has expanded into many more product areas, all themed around extreme sports, including hotels, travel, mobile phones and pre-pay cards. Despite this tremendous growth, Al Gosling gives the sense that this is still just the start of something which will grow very much larger.

HARGREAVES LANSDOWN

Hargreaves Lansdown

The Power in Being Proactive

Company:	**Hargreaves Lansdown**	
Founders:	**Peter Hargreaves and Stephen Lansdown**	
Age at start:	**34 and 28**	
Background:	**Both chartered accountants working in investment management**	
Start year:	**1981**	
Business:	**Independent financial advisor**	

Hargreaves Lansdown was founded in 1981 by chartered accountants Peter Hargreaves and Stephen Lansdown. Since its inception the business has grown substantially and steadily into one of the leading Independent Investment Brokers in the country today. By the end of June 2006 the company was managing about £1 billion; mainly individuals' savings. In addition to this they administer another £8 billion or so on behalf of 200,000 investors. The business employs about 650 people, and has a turnover of £70 million.

Grounded in Experience

Peter and Stephen had known most of their lives that they wanted to run their own business, but they admit that had they not grown restless with their nine to five jobs, they very likely never would have taken the plunge into entrepreneurship. Peter explains that had their previous employer kept himself out of financial difficulties and paid them a sensible salary, the chances are they would still be there and Hargreaves Lansdown would still be just an idea in the back of their minds.

'Most entrepreneurs were forced into business through either losing their job, lack of respect for their boss or the failure of the firm in which they worked.'

Peter reasons that most aspiring entrepreneurs never follow through on their business ideas because they are comfortable where they sit. 'I only know one entrepreneur who actually, in a premeditated way, planned his new business and exited from a well-paid job,' he says. 'Most entrepreneurs were forced into business through either losing their job, lack of respect for their boss or the failure of the firm in which they worked.'

The founders were both qualified chartered accountants who had moved to work in investment management. They both joined a small firm in Bristol but soon realised that the organisation was not being run very efficiently and that it might not last for very long. Peter eventually left and briefly courted a firm which was targeting consumers directly. Peter thought that he could do a better job and asked Stephen to join him and they set up one of the country's first 'marketing-driven' investment brokerage firms,

Co-founder Peter Hargreaves.

Co-founder Stephen Lansdown.

selling products such as unit trusts to savers by direct mail, rather than the traditional, more expensive route of sending a sales person to call on potential savers.

To launch their brokerage they would need to get around the huge obstacle that was their anonymity. In an industry which depended on trust and was dominated by time-tested, reliable names, no one would know theirs. But Peter and Stephen felt they had recognized something no one else in their industry had seemed to catch onto, and that was the emerging power of targeted marketing. While there were many firms providing a competent, professional service, it was largely impersonal. Most companies were sales-driven, and Peter and Stephen sensed a disconnect that was both wasting companies' time and limiting their client base.

'Using the traditional sales-driven business model, companies sent a salesman along when anyone wanted investment advice,' Peter says. 'But because the product we wanted to provide was essentially investing in the stock market, clients were very cautious. Each sales person could see several potential clients, yet many of these decided to do nothing. This means that the average salesman makes many calls for each sale, and it is not unreasonable to suggest that the people who do proceed pay for the time spent dealing with the ones who don't.' By taking a direct marketing approach, therefore, Peter and Stephen thought they could achieve sales at considerably lower costs than the existing brokerages.

In spring 1981, the situation at their employer had worsened, and Stephen and Peter found themselves the only staff left other than the founder – and they became increasingly concerned. Their knowledge of the sector convinced them that there was a substantial opportunity, while their belief in the plan never made the financial risks of starting up feel as precarious as they might outwardly seem.

'He decided that he could afford to give the business six months to start paying him a sustainable wage.'

So on July 1 1981, they started a business and named it after themselves – Hargreaves Lansdown. Peter and Stephen each had a car and introduced a few hundred pounds into the company at the outset to get it started, and they ran the business from a small office in Peter's home, with just a part-time secretary to help them. Stephen perhaps risked more personally at the time as he had only around £2,000 in a building society and a wife who was seven months pregnant. Stephen recalls that, aged 27, he decided that he could afford to give the business six months to start paying him a sustainable wage, otherwise he would have to find another job.

Setting Up the Business

Their first task was to register as agents with the major unit trust companies – at the time M&G, Save and Prosper, Henderson, and Gartmore – so that if they made some sales these companies would pay them a commission. Commission for agents was 1.25%, plus an extra 1.75% for marketing. (These days, selling financial services products is far more regulated). Once they were registered they were in the position to start seeking their first clients. To start with they decided to continue selling the traditional way, to get funds flowing in quickly while they started their direct marketing approach. So they contacted accountancy and solicitors' firms, promoting their new business on the back of their chartered accountancy qualification and their recent experience. They also focussed on selling unit trusts, which new legislation had just made very tax efficient compared to insurance bonds, which most brokers at the time promoted, as they paid higher commissions.

Impressively they won their first two clients very quickly – one brought in each by

Peter and Stephen – which made the company a cash-generative business from its first month of trading.

Rather than waiting for clients to make the first contact, the pair developed a simple strategy to market to their audience. 'The plan was to send them lots of information and suggestions and allow them to make up their own minds,' Peter explains. 'This meant that we didn't have to pay expensive sales people, and more importantly, we could be very selective about who we market to and could quickly and easily adjust our marketing effort and budget commensurate with investor confidence.'

'What's more, if you post your marketing literature you can contact as many potential clients as the size of your list. We had one, single plan – to have the most names and addresses of potential investors in the UK.'

'Our strategy was simply to advertise what people wanted.'

They began their new marketing approach by placing a small advertisement in a weekend edition of a national newspaper, about a month after setting up. Stephen remembers well that they had a hard time persuading the paper to run the advertisement, since he hadn't heard of their business. 'We actually only advertised for people who were interested in buying unit trusts,' Peter recalls. 'Indeed, the headline of our advert read, 'Choosing A Unit Trust?' Our strategy was simply to advertise what people wanted.' And it seems this strategy worked for them. 'We got 168 responses from our first advert,' notes Peter, 'and I knew the moment I saw the post that we were going to be fantastically successful.'

Indeed, unlike many of the startup businesses in this book, the company was profitable after just three months, and it has been ever since. Returns from Peter's client, the second to invest, injected enough cash into the fledgling brokerage to purchase an early home computer with a word processing program and a much-needed printer. Very few companies in 1981 had a word processor, Peter recalls, and it proved to be a very astute use of their limited resources. The word processor's organisational capabilities paid for itself every two months in that first year of operations. Their early success was crucial, he believes, in establishing the company and setting the pace and tone of its future operations. 'We have never had to introduce any further working capital,' Peter says.

So why was this business so successful, so fast? 'We believe the investing public prefer buying investment products by direct mail because they don't like being pressurised by having a sales person in front of them. They like to make up their own minds as and when they feel they wish to commit more capital to investment,' he adds.

Continually Improving

While their initial success came from solicitors and accountants, as their client list grew throughout their first year, Peter and Stephen both shared a commitment to plough almost all the money they made back into marketing, taking out as wages only what they needed to survive. They redoubled their advertising efforts and constantly reviewed the effectiveness of their ads, improving them over time. The pair looked at how they could maintain their average marketing spend yet make their advertisements stand out more. One solution was to change their standard 'five double' ads – an advert that runs across two columns, five centimetres deep – into a '10 single', which featured more prominently on the page.

Other efforts included taking distress and last-minute space at various publications. 'The newspapers soon got to know that they could talk to somebody here at five o'clock and get an answer,' Peter says, pointing out that they have been able to cut out the costs of advertising agencies by teaching themselves the tenets of marketing over the years.

But their strategy had other productive elements to it. A strong belief in communicating with clients motivated the launch of a regular newsletter, *The Unit Investor,* as early as October in their first year. This was instantly very popular, and continues today as an important, extremely popular, communication tool. Today the newsletter is called *The Investment Times* and is Europe's most widely read specialist investment newsletter.

'We benchmarked against other people's models until we felt we were the best.'

They took a proactive strategy toward developing their marketing, constantly reviewing and improving their literature. 'We benchmarked against other people's models until we felt we were the best, and then every time we produced new literature we did so with the goal of making it better than our previous attempt,' Hargreaves says. 'We would clarify the English, improve the layout or revamp the content. We still do that today. 'Improvement is vital in all business. You can guarantee that everybody else competing with you is improving, and if you stand still they will eventually sneak up and overtake you.'

Their business has been driven by marketing, and from the very beginning, even whilst operating from a spare bedroom in Peter's small mews house, they understood it was important to maintain that small company atmosphere. A simple part of this was answering their phone when clients called. While they embraced new technology such as word processors, they stepped back from the trend toward automated answering systems. The pair made an agreement that Stephen would schedule appointments on odd days of the month, while Peter kept his to the even days. The partner with no appointments in his diary would man the phones.

'The most important thing for anyone starting a business is to find out what your clients want and provide it to them,' Peter explains. 'Don't try and give them what you think they want.'

Peter says that despite a firm belief early on in their marketing model, they really didn't expect the business to take off quite as much, quite so quickly. They presumed they would operate from their original premises for a couple of years, but after nine months, he says it was clear their operation had grown too big for Peter's spare bedroom.

'Within 18 months of taking our second premises we realised we needed to move again,' Peter recalls. 'I certainly think we probably did more than twice the business we expected in every one of the first five years. Initially we were doubling every three months. The only time things nearly got out of hand was at the height of the bull market that ended in October 1987. We debated during that summer whether we had the capacity to handle the business if we continued marketing.' In fact by the time the crash hit in 1987, they had diversified into insurance broking as well, which, coupled with their flexible approach and cost structure, helped them survive the next two, lean years at the brokerage.

When Peter and Stephen started it was Stephen's wish that they would be the best and Peter's wish that they would be the biggest. Within two years Peter realised you would never be the biggest unless you were the best. Today they have arguably achieved both goals. Peter adds reflectively: 'We just needed £1 million worth of unit trust business a year to survive. Today we handle £2 billion worth per annum. We dreamt big but we never grew too fast. We could always handle the growth.'

WHERE ARE THEY NOW?

Peter Hargreaves and Stephen Lansdown's once unknown brokerage now stands out as one of the sector's most trusted names. Hargreaves Lansdown now employs around 650 staff across its six, chief operating divisions. And 25 successful years have not left its founders detached: they remain committed to the continued innovation of their company's services and make it a point not to let that small business feeling escape them. Peter is now the Chief Executive, focussed on expanding the business, and Stephen the Chairman, focussed on continued strong delivery of their services.

VITABIOTICS
WHERE NATURE MEETS SCIENCE

Vitabiotics

Supplementing the Healthcare Market

Company:	**Vitabiotics**
Founders:	**Dr Lalvani and Dr Meyer**
Age at start:	**Dr Lalvani 36**
Background:	**Pharmacist / Scientist**
Start year:	**1971**
Business:	**Healthcare product manufacturer**

Scientist **Dr Lalvani founded Vitabiotics** with colleague Dr Meyer in 1971 after personal research into mouth ulcer remedies flagged up a serious gap in the medicinal market for alternative, nutrient therapies. After initial struggles to get the single treatment (rather than a series of products) sold in small pharmacies, the company now sells £55 million worth of 20 different brands to UK supermarkets and pharmaceutical outlets nationwide.

An Inspirational Problem

Although Dr Lalvani had entertained vague notions of running his own business prior to the creation of Vitabiotics, like many successful businesses the company grew from a single idea. After moving to London in 1956, having gained a degree in pharmacy and a doctorate in medicinal chemistry and working part-time at weekends as a pharmacist, Dr Lalvani first hit on the idea of a new concept in mouth ulcer treatment when, having suffered from persistent mouth ulcers himself, he realised there weren't any really effective treatments and the market was in need of an alternative remedy. In 1963 Dr Lalvani found what he thought was the solution; he tested it on himself – and it worked. Next, Dr Lalvani, who took a short-term role as a Research Fellow at the AIIMS Medical college in Delhi, was able to test the product on around 30 mouth ulcer patients over the next few years; the results were highly impressive, and in due course Dr Lalvani applied and obtained a patent in 1968, as a legal protection for his invention, being the first such treatment with combined antifungal and antibacterial function besides vitamin C.

As with many entrepreneurs early on, struggling financial costs meant that Dr Lalvani had to put his business idea on hold for a number of years while he saved up enough cash to foot the cost of further research. He made the best of this by spending the next three years saving up money from his pharmacist wage whilst also ensuring he kept on top of scientific developments in the areas of nutrients and vitamins. As a result, by 1971, when he was 36 years old, he had £6,000 worth of savings and a working knowledge of nutrient therapy; he invested it all in a new business to market his newly patented mouth ulcer treatment.

To start with, Dr Lalvani tried to licence Oralcer to big companies who could produce it and sell it on to pharmacies and retail outlets far more easily than he could, since they already had manufacturing and sales operations up and running. He soon realised, however, that they didn't see the potential for his product that he believed was there, so Dr Lalvani decided instead to set up his own company and sell the product directly. He and research colleague Dr Meyer called the new company Vitabiotics.

Slow and Steady Wins the Race

As all entrepreneurs know, initial sales for a new product from a new company are never easy. Making the first sale is necessary and an enormous step for virtually any business, and in Spring 1971 Dr Lalvani succeeded in making his first sale of approximately five pounds of Oralcer to a local London pharmacy using his pharmaceutical background and knowledge of the product to convince the buyers of its worth. As well as this, he confides, he also embarked on the unusual though effective marketing strategy of trying to convince pharmacies verbally to recommend Oralcer to their customers who had failed to benefit from previous treatment. Not only did this save him the cost of advertising to consumers, but also it gave a direct and personal touch to the product, with Dr Lalvani using his knowledge of the product to explain just why it would be a valuable alternative to other similar goods available to the consumer.

'*He embarked on the unusual marketing strategy of trying to convince pharmacies verbally to recommend Oralcer to their customers.*'

And the product succeeded, albeit slowly, proving itself to be a worthy alternative treatment. Within a year after the Oralcer launch, Dr Lalvani was now ready for launching Britain's first specialised multi nutrient vitamin product, branded as Omega-H3. After taking on his first member of staff – a friend who happened to be looking for a job and who could assist with the admin – Dr Lalvani spent another few months approaching pharmacies in the area before investing further some of his £6,000 into placing a number of small advertisements in trade publications such as *The Chemist and Druggist* and *The Pharmaceutical Journal*. This highly targeted marketing paid off, and by the end of the first year around 800 pharmacies were stocking Oralcer.

Dr Lalvani then extended his investment for small ads in mainstream consumer publications, using newspapers such as the *The Express* and *The Mirror* in the hope that the profile of Vitabiotics would be raised and a productive second and third year could be ensured.

This early UK promotion, Dr Lalvani admits, was a struggle – with the costs of the second batch of advertising taking almost all of Oralcer's sales revenue. Luckily, though, the business came across 'a good export opportunity' midway through the first year for his newly introduced vitamin product, and this allowed them to carry on investing heavily in advertising. One of Dr Lalvani's friends, who was at that time working in Nigeria, told him that there was strong potential to export vitamins there. Dr Lalvani took his advice, looked into it, and sold there very successfully. Vitamins were in high demand and Omega-H3 was the first beautifully packaged vitamin product offering high quality and researched vitamins with ginseng – it instantly appealed to consumers.

Vitabiotics has done more and more export business ever since, winning a Queen's Award for Excellence in International Trade in May 2003. Now, exports to 70 countries worldwide make up half the company's sales.

Meanwhile, Dr Lalvani continued to invest for further research into nutrient combinations that catered to a variety of health needs. This led to new discoveries which Vitabiotics transformed into speciality vitamin supplements such as Pregnacare, Osteocare and Menopace. This time, though, Dr Lalvani decided not to do the experiments and later stages of research himself, partly because he was too busy launching the new business, and partly due to the increasing complexity of nutrient

'Never stop believing in your idea even if your early returns do not reflect what you believe to be the true potential of your product.'

combinations; instead, he commissioned other researchers to come up with the precise formula, offering the information he had discovered from his personal interest in nutrition and pharmaceuticals to scientists who could then test and ultimately produce a working supplement.

Looking back over the first year, Dr Lalvani admits that it did not achieve his expectations, with total sales figures reaching a rather humble £7,000 (the equivalent of about £68,000 today). He did not get too discouraged by this, however, and now advises budding entrepreneurs to never stop believing in their idea even if their early returns do not reflect the true potential of a product.

For the first few years after the launch of Oralcer, the company invested steadily more in vitamin and nutrient research, funded mainly from export revenue from Omega-H3 and partly by the slow but consistent rise in the popularity of Oralcer. It took six years after Oralcer and Omega-H3's launch, before Vitabiotics' most advanced range of nutrient based treatments were successfully launched for specific health areas.

Although multi vitamins are now established and commonly available, when Vitabiotics launched Omega-H3, it was a completely new concept. It sold well abroad almost immediately, but was slower to take off in Britain. After a few years Britain caught on, though, growing Vitabiotics' turnover considerably and further establishing the company as an innovative developer and producer of 'nutrient technology'. More and more testimonials from happy customers poured in, and the company was increasingly covered in the media, which led to a fresh influx of interest.

Targeting The Market

Patience is a virtue with business and Dr Lalvani is a big believer in waiting for the right product to come along. For a long time he waited for a really big product, one that in his eyes 'would truly benefit people'. Sixteen years after the launch of Omega-H3, and 18 years after launching its original product, Vitabiotics were instrumental

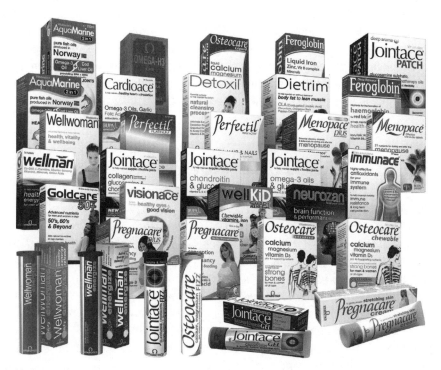

Vitabiotics' product range today.

in developing a market for vitamins that worked in individual, specific areas such as supplements aimed at pregnant women or those going through menopause, for joint health, skincare and memory.

Dr Lalvani's business team approached the high-street chemist Boots with the ideas for their two new products Menopace® and Premence® not long before their launch in 1992, but were turned away as Boots wanted to see evidence of a market for the products. Disappointed but not deterred, Vitabiotics decided to establish the products by first selling through health food stores. It also focussed on verifying the benefits of the new products through highly successful clinical trials.

One year after the products were launched to much acclaim, Boots could see there was a market and agreed to stock them. Many other large-scale distribution channels such as Superdrug, Tesco and Safeway followed suit soon afterwards, eventually creating their own specialist products in the same vein.

Since then, through continued research and ongoing success with clinical trials, Vitabiotics have gone from strength to strength. In 2001, Vitabiotics' product Visionace became the first micronutrient product ever to show highly significant results in treating marginal dry eye syndrome and in 2004, Dr Lalvani won the Innovation Award from the DTI Minister of Science, after the ground breaking publication on the significant effects of Immunace tablets on mortality outcomes. In 2007 the Integrative Medicine Insights journal published the results of the benefit of his Diabetone vitamin capsules in the general well being of type II diabetic patients. In fact, Vitabiotics is the only company in the nutraceutical field with so many products that have demonstrated their effectiveness during orthodox clinical trials and which have opened up whole new areas of nutrient medicine.

WHERE ARE THEY NOW?

Although Dr Lalvani has delegated some of the responsibility for the company to Vitabiotics' now strong management team, which includes his son, Tej Lalvani and Director Robert Taylor, together with his eldest son, non-executive Medical Director Professor Ajit Lalvani, he is still very much involved with the company and shows no sign of slowing as he gets older.

Vitabiotics expanded onto the web in 2000 and now exports to 85 countries worldwide with 20 brands in the UK alone, eight of which are number one in their own individual category. It has been successful in breaking into the lucrative US healthcare market, and is now focussed on building up existing brands by creating new ranges of products.

Jigsaw Research

Jigsaw Research

A New Model of Market Research

Company:	**Jigsaw Research**
Founders:	**Ann Morgan, Sue Van Meeteren and Jo McDonald**
Age at start:	**35, 36 and 29**
Background:	**Ann and Sue had a background in market research and worked at Research International together for seven years. Jo was their PA.**
Start year:	**1998**
Business:	**Market research agency**

J igsaw Research is a small, quality-focussed market research company based in central London. From its conception, its client list included American Express, Shell and Price Waterhouse Coopers. The company's founders left the market research giant, Research International, to start from scratch, replacing bureaucracy and board meetings with a balance of home and egalitarianism. Eight years on, Jigsaw is firmly established and respected in the market research field. It has grown steadily since it was founded and now consists of 16 director-level staff and has a turnover of around £4 million. It is a unique company, individual in its approach, and sets itself apart as a small fish in a big pond.

Bureaucratic Allergy

Managing director Sue Van Meeteren and her deputy Ann Morgan had worked at Research International (RI) together for seven years. They were members of the UK board of directors and were as influential as they could be in the context of a company which was part of a larger group. Yet both were fed up being stuck in internal meetings all day, having no actual contact with their clients. Determined to leave, Ann and Sue had to make a decision: do they join another leading agency with which they may experience similar problems, or brave it and establish a brand new agency?

With a fair amount of confidence and supported by encouragement from some of their existing clients that they would get business quickly, they decided to try a new model of a market research agency. Jo McDonald, their current PA, had also just left RI and encouraged them to start a company rather than operate as freelancers. Jo was to become invaluable when they were starting the company. The market was full of big agencies which Ann adds 'were not doing a very good job' so they felt there was room for a small company which focused more single-mindedly on its clients' needs. Indeed, clients had previously complained to them that they were not satisfied with the larger agencies' approach to their accounts and wanted greater access to more senior researchers.

'The founders aimed to be directly involved in client accounts.'

So, 'allergic' to anything bureaucratic, the founders aimed to be directly involved in client accounts and decided not to employ trainees or juniors. This was a pretty groundbreaking idea and solved a problem often encountered at their previous company: all too often, experienced, senior staff were tied up with management tasks, so clients mainly dealt with less experienced junior staff and were left feeling unsatisfied with their level of expertise. If the juniors got something wrong, senior management would then have to step in, sort out the problem and spend time pacifying the client. Without this risk, Jigsaw ensured their clients would always receive the best service from the most experienced people and service would not fall into the pattern they had formerly experienced. They intended to only employ people who were experienced and good at their jobs, so they could work relatively independently and produce excellent results every time.

Before she and Sue started Jigsaw, Ann recalls clients asking to work with her, but never being able to because of her management role. At Jigsaw, Ann would be able to get stuck into client work without corporate restraints. From a commercial perspective, Ann and Sue knew this model would appeal to clients who were frustrated with the bigger companies. The research market was 'inundated with big, lumbering companies' who were often difficult to access and provided inconsistent quality. Clients did not know which department they need or no one answered the phone. Jigsaw appealed to clients with their small, personal operation.

A New Approach

Although there were other small market research companies, Sue and Ann soon established themselves as unique. They tackled the two main types of research, qualitative and quantitative, to provide clients with a seamless and complete offer. While small companies specialising in qualitative research were quite common, Jigsaw offered an integrated service. As well as the qualitative side, they also designed and ran larger quantitative studies involving large samples. This positioning was unusual in the market where most smaller agencies only specialised in one type of research.

Sue and Ann had impeccable experience in their field and were confident in their ability to perform. Ann had joined MORI (Marketing Opinion Research International) in 1985 as a graduate trainee and in 1988 began on the second rung of the career ladder at RI. She was promoted with the wave of company growth and was made a divisional director by the age of 28. Sue had a degree in Business Studies and begun her career working at IBM for a few years after graduating. She was made head of research at National and Provincial Building Society when she was only 25, and joined Ann at RI as a director in 1992. With this impressive CV behind them, as long as they did not price themselves too highly, they were confident clients would follow them if they set up on their own.

The motivation to begin their own business was further spurred by changes in their personal circumstances. It was a time of radical change for the pair when they moved from working 12-hour plus days in the thick of company politics to becoming mothers. Ann left RI in July 1998, the same month in which Sue had her second child. By November that year, when Sue was ready to go back to work, Ann had fallen pregnant with her first child, but was eager to found the company nevertheless.

'We weren't trying to take on the world.'

Ann stresses that at the beginning, their ambitions were very low-key. They certainly 'weren't trying to take on the world'. Their goal was to generate a decent amount of business, have some good clients on the books and do a good job for them. Without corporate restraint, they could take control and decide their own growth rate. If they wanted to take more time to focus on family life and concentrate less on expanding, or if they wanted to take on a small or charitable client who would not be very profitable, they could.

Jigsaw's current offices in Margaret Street, central London.

Despite all these benefits, there were also compromises to be made when making this career change. While they wanted to continue to be mums, Ann notes that she did find the drop in status difficult at first. From their position at the top of a complex hierarchy, she describes the stark contrast of finding herself sitting around wondering if a client might phone them. The prestige and professional self-esteem that they were used to had vanished.

They also found that they had to make big financial sacrifices for a number of years. They both found this 'huge trade off' quite difficult to adjust to, but agree now that, 'the advantages massively outweighed the disadvantages'.

The startup capital for the business was not as big as some, about £40,000, and they were able to fund this from personal savings; therefore, managing to avoid taking on an overdraft or bank loan. They were careful to keep their overheads low at the beginning, only spending on what they perceived to be essesntials such as serviced office space, computers and a letterhead. Through doing so they were able to pay themselves back the startup capital of £40,000 within the first couple of years, however their salaries remained suppressed for longer.

A Business and Baby Boom

Jigsaw Research was formally founded in November 1998, a few months after Sue and Ann had left RI. Within three months Jigsaw had a few crucial client names under its belt: it won business from American Express, Shell and PriceWaterhouse Coopers. These had all been clients of Sue and Ann's, and the founders had known that these companies were looking for alternative suppliers. Jigsaw offered them an alternative arrangement to work with. While these names sound intimidating for a small company, Ann explains the projects were relatively small – anything from three weeks to three months in duration – and so were well within the founders' capabilities. They only needed three clients who trusted them to give them a chance with some small projects to get started and lay the foundations from which to build.

'Word-of-mouth and who-you-know are both crucial in winning business.'

There was no need for them to do any marketing at all, although they did set up a website early on. All their initial work came from previous contacts and then subsequently from word of mouth referrals. Ann admits that the company name, Jigsaw Research, was not sufficiently well known to attract clients in the early years and it is only now, nine years on, that they are beginning to acquire significant brand presence. Because the market research world is fairly small, word-of-mouth and who-you-know are both crucial in winning business. It was their reputation that preceded them and previous contacts that won them work.

While Sue and Ann focused on winning and doing work for their new clients, Jo was fundamental in setting up the administration and financial side of the business. Sue and Ann had had experience of running large departments and had been very involved in financial management, but without Jo, they could not have concentrated solely on client work, and carried out their model. She embraced the new challenge at Jigsaw, taking control of the administrative needs of the new organisation, putting in place invoicing and accounting systems which Jigsaw has slightly adapted since but largely still uses to this day. Sue and Ann gave Jo the space to learn and teach herself, so that now, Ann describes her as 'a sort of unofficial Financial Director, but with Operations and Facilities Manager also being part of her fairly taxing job description!'. They got some help from an accountant, but tried to limit the use in order to keep costs down. Without Jo's help, Ann doubts the birth of Jigsaw would have been as smooth. She describes bringing Jo with them as 'the single most sensible thing we did'. Having good support can make or break a company, she warns.

Although the early months were successful, Jigsaw did not get off to an ideal start, given Ann's early stages of pregnancy: having won the work, they then needed someone to cover for Ann when she went on maternity leave. This forced them to recruit earlier than perhaps they would have done. Sarah McKee, a friend and ex-colleague approached them pretty much as soon as they started. Ann describes the 'gamble' they took in taking on an employee so early on when they were yet to establish themselves firmly. She recalls Sarah's father asking his daughter for Jigsaw's business plan, which was non-existent. She admits 'it must sound bizarre but we really knew it would be OK'. Sarah started in early March, a week before Ann started her maternity leave.

They recruited again in June, following much the same process of taking on a previous colleague who had approached them. She had also been on maternity leave and did not bring any clients with her, but Sue and Ann trusted in her outstanding ability. Recruitment policy remained very much 'who do we know, who is good and who has expressed an interest in working with us again?' By the end of the first year, Jigsaw had grown to five employees, all previous colleagues or contacts.

Unexpected Animosity

When Ann and Sue left RI, they had no idea how much ruction this would end up causing. Their former employer became concerned about the potential damage it feared Jigsaw was doing to it, and reacted. One course of action RI took was contact all its clients and ask them not to give work to Jigsaw. At the time it was usual practice for third party agencies to use RI's international branches for overseas research. However, when Jigsaw made contact with local offices, they found they were banned from using them. More baffled than seriously affected, Ann and Sue forged new relationships with independent international agencies, which was achievable but made a simple process more complex.

Jigsaw's founders tried to assure RI that they were not out either to steal clients or to damage RI by creating a rival company. Their small ambitions and intention to 'ply our trade in a quiet way' posed no material threat to the large company. Yet nevertheless it seemed that RI felt in some way threatened by Jigsaw.

By the end of the first year, they had made a name for themselves among the clients as a company who produced results quickly. Ann describes Jigsaw as 'a nimble, boutique operation', which was able to act quickly in comparison with the juggernaut agencies that would take ages to get going on a project.

'If you're decent and get the basics right, it's possible to do well.'

The business performed well and the founders were able to pay their employees market salaries although they themselves took less money than they could have earned working for another research firm; they even had a bit left over for a bonus. Without a hierarchy, Jigsaw was run on an egalitarian basis. Ann describes the 'very informal' process of deciding bonuses in the early days, sitting round a table and discussing how much they thought each should get. The success of their first year was commendable, yet Ann, in common with many entrepreneurs, humbly protests 'it's not that difficult a market. If you're decent and get the basics right, it's possible to do well'. She emphasises that it is important to focus on your product and resist the temptation to become distracted and rush your growth.

From the beginning, the company operated in a very relaxed way. The founders comment that while people expect new businesses to require long hours and sleepless nights, Jigsaw's startup was remarkably low-key and very easy going. 'It's a huge market and we were only trying to nibble away and get a little bit of it,' notes Ann. She describes it as 'friends sitting round, working in a collaborative way'. Later, they started to reorganise themselves in a more conventional way, but for the first few years, they grew fast without planned expansion and there was no need for rigid structure.

WHERE ARE THEY NOW?

All three founders remain in their respective posts in the company. Jigsaw has grown into an established and successful medium-sized research business. It intends to expand at a rate of 15% a year, which the founders believe they can achieve without compromising their core principles, focussing on client care and excellent service.

Pimlico Plumbers

Common Sense Ain't That Common

Company:	**Pimlico Plumbers**
Founders:	**Charlie Mullins**
Age at start:	**27**
Background:	**Plumber by trade**
Start year:	**1979**
Business:	**Plumbers**

Pimlico Plumbers sprung from humble beginnings. As a nine-year-old boy, founder Charlie Mullins bunked off school to earn 'two bob' a time helping out his local Camden plumber. His company now earns over £14 million per year with a client list that includes the likes of Jonathan Ross, Eric Clapton, Louis Theroux, Boy George, Michael Winner and Tara Palmer Tomkinson. It turned the plumbing industry on its head, creating a reputable brand bursting with reliable, trustworthy plumbers.

The straight-talking pioneer describes his London-based company as 'the complete opposite' of stereotypical plumbers who have disappointed in the past. Charlie's main concern was to shed the image of an unreliable rogue, a feat that took years to achieve. Thirty years ago, plumbing was by no means trendy; now it is practically cool. Charlie is Britain's first millionaire plumber and has differentiated his business enough that he has inspired a new generation of plumbing companies.

The seeds were sown very young, a factor which Charlie attributes to his success. Inspired by a local plumber because he drove a Ford Zephyr and seemed to be the richest person in the area, Charlie had a working and in-depth knowledge of plumbing before he was 10 years old. Since then, his whole working life has involved plumbing and so when it came to starting out on his own, he was in a position to note all the things which customers disliked. The public were fed up of plumbers arriving late, cancelling appointments and turning up badly presented, all of which were perceived to be plumbing industry standards.

New Expectations

These days, the general public realise they do not need to stand for shoddy work or cowboys. The smell of lawsuits and customer rights hang in the air. Charlie very simply did the complete opposite of what was perceived and used this as a simple yet highly effective way of distinguishing his business from other plumbers. He comments that 'you either improve your service or don't become a busy company'. Arriving well presented, on time, and doing a good job are milestones in promoting a different image of the plumbing industry. Only in the last decade or so that plumbing has been truly viewed as different. Pimlico Plumbers has paved the way for this change.

Proud of his ambitious attitude, which he feels set him apart from his contemporaries, Charlie took this working idea forward, making the most of opportunities when they arose. He believes plumbers are not necessarily forward-thinking people and this is perhaps why a more concerted business plan was not attempted earlier. By using his common sense and making the most of opportunities, Charlie began to build his plumbing empire pipe by pipe.

Charlie deems common sense (which he believes is not as 'common' as many presume) an essential quality for any successful businessman. By this, he means an

Charlie and one of Pimlico's well-known vans.

> '*Everybody thinks they have common sense, but the problem is it ain't common.*'

alert, on-the-ball attitude that made *him* take a normal plumbing business to the next level. The problem is, 'unfortunately, they all think they have common sense, don't they?'

Organic Growth

Charlie left school with no qualifications, and went straight into a four-year plumbing apprenticeship, following in the footsteps of his local plumber hero. After this, he began working for himself. He chose never to work for a company, as he disliked building sites and wanted to be his own boss. Thus the only option was to become self employed, build up a client base and create a good reputation.

Pimlico Plumbers' call centre in Pimlico House, central London.

More and more of Charlie's clients were based around London's Pimlico area, and in 1979 while he was working out of the basement of an estate agent called Pimlico Properties, he chose his company's name. It seemed a logical step, as he did not need to venture further into London to make a living. Even now, Pimlico mainly operates in a five-mile radius covering the Central London areas of Kensington, Chelsea and Belgravia.

His ethos of time keeping and honesty went a long way in London's demanding and unforgiving marketplace. Yet his youth and seeming inexperience proved problematic when convincing clients he was 'legit'. Some discarded his four years of training too quickly and the bad reputation of plumbers preceded him. Charlie remembers that in the early years, in order to win some jobs, he insisted that no payment was made until the job was completed to the customer's absolute satisfaction.

'Once it gets moving, your reputation can get you somewhere before you get there.'

Pimlico Plumbers did not become a household name overnight. Nor did Charlie employ permanent staff for a few years. Friends would help him with jobs on a larger scale, so that 'once people know you are more than a one-man-band, they offer you the bigger job'. This is how Pimlico set up. There were no investors, bank loans or business strategies. The business was self-funding and expanded when it had the money to do so. Its reputation was created by word-of mouth; 'it takes a long time to spread. But eventually, once it gets moving, your reputation can get you somewhere before you get there,' notes Charlie.

From the beginning, Charlie strove to offer a 24/7 service. As he was the only plumber of the 'company', this facility was not as guaranteed as it is today, but Charlie always tried to work to this policy. Over the years, Pimlico has endeavoured to create a more reliable service than its competitors and now guarantees their 24-hour availability and to have someone with the customer within the hour if necessary.

Charlie did not have high expectations for Pimlico's founding years; its aim was simply to be continually busy. In the first year, Charlie earned enough to pay himself a wage and buy a second hand van from auction. Charlie is very much into the 'gradual' and allowed the business to grow organically, without forcing anything. Indeed, without ever having a rigid business plan, Pimlico Plumbers undoubtedly relied on the relentless need for plumbers coupled with principles of reliability and integrity to generate and keep business. Today, almost 80% of Pimlico's workload is generated from people who have used them before.

'Reputation takes a long while to build up but you can lose it overnight.'

Charlie is vehement that Pimlico has never and will never have outside investors. He acknowledges that whilst the business could have been 10 times bigger and probably national if he had taken on investors, it may not have been better. He does not want to lose control of the company. As Pimlico established itself, Charlie did receive a number of offers of investment, but his concern was for Pimlico's reputation. 'Reputation takes a long while to build up and yet you can lose it overnight. We are the company we are because we provide the service when people want the service.'

Plumbing Prejudice

After the first couple of years, the business began advertising in the local paper, the *Westminster and Pimlico Informer*, but was not permitted space on the front-page to begin with. Charlie believes this was because of the stigma attached to plumbers. Over the years, Pimlico Plumbers has slowly been promoted from being lost amongst the pages to claiming a front-page spot, a progression they are very proud of. Having fought for this position, Charlie certainly will not part with it.

While leaking taps, bathroom floods and, in the last decade, a property renovation boom meant there was always work, like any other business, Pimlico Plumbers had obstacles to tackle. Finding the right premises at the right price and in the right location was a struggle. As with advertising, Charlie believes he faced 'plumbing prejudice' when seeking premises, as landlords were reluctant to let to plumbers. Charlie recognised the need to take on highly visible, prominent premises, and admits companies who work in 'tiny little backstreet places where nobody knows of them' baffle him. The first place Pimlico operated from was in the heart of Pimlico. Now, they are prominently based in Lambeth.

Keep it Simple

From small beginnings to the company's present day success, managing more than 1,200 jobs a week, Charlie emphasises the need to keep it simple. Some may find his manner blunt and he certainly takes pride in a no-nonsense attitude to business, not letting himself be swayed by swanky titles and complicated presentations that he feels are surplus to requirements. Surprisingly, he has never met his bank manager, and admits he does not even know their name. In fact, he detests meetings of any kind and will go out of his way to avoid them. That is how Pimlico has always been run – on a need-to-know, straightforward basis.

He has, however, followed a lucid marketing campaign, which he believes is crucial for any business, combining adverts in the *Yellow Pages* with prominent premises signage and smart, well maintained and highly branded vans, which have become well known around London – helped by the introduction of cheeky number plates, such as LOO2OLD and BOG1.

WHERE ARE THEY NOW?

Now aged 54, Charlie Mullins is still very involved in Pimlico Plumbers; he remains energetic and ambitious for both his company and the plumbing industry. He aims to encourage more women to take up the profession and is still actively involved in transforming it into a more reputable, popular profession.

Although Pimlico does not intend to develop outside the M25, it is nevertheless expanding. Pimlico Home Services Group was set up in 2000 to meet customer demand for a range of domestic property services including carpentry, electrical work, repair and maintenance of home appliances, tiling and decorating.

Glasses Direct

A Clear Vision

Company:	**Glasses Direct**
Founders:	**James Murray-Wells**
Age at start:	**21**
Background:	**Student**
Start year:	**2004**
Business:	**Online glasses retailer**

Glasses Direct has probably had more column inches in the national press over the last 18 months than any other business in this book, despite being just a few years old. Its impressive press coverage is due to the fact that one man decided to take on an entire industry, and seems to be winning. It is a story of justice and triumph of 'the little guy' over corporate giants, made all the more appealing by the fact that its founder was a student when he set up the business, which is now selling millions of pounds worth of glasses every year.

Shocked into Action

James Murray-Wells was just 21 when the idea for Glasses Direct came to him, studying English at the University of the West of England, Bristol. Despite his youth, James already had a keen business mind and had been looking for business opportunities for years when he came up with the idea for Glasses Direct. He was adept at IT and had developed an interest in 'the way the Internet was heading'; he confesses that he saw university as a good time to look out for business ideas that might work online. 'As universities generally (and English degrees in particular!) bought with them a lot of free time as well as good support networks, they provide a great launch pad for starting a business,' explains James.

One day he learned that he needed reading glasses for the first time (which he puts down to too much reading, primarily Harry Potter) and was shocked by how expensive glasses were. Even the frames alone often cost over £100, while the total price of a pair of glasses could easily reach several hundred pounds. Realising that the high-street prices simply had to be too much money for what was essentially 'some wire and some glass', James felt sure that there must be a dramatic mark up on the manufacturers cost to the opticians, which meant that a web-based business could offer customers a much better deal and still make good money.

So James started work researching the manufacturing costs of a pair of glasses. Trawling internet forums and chatting online to people in the trade, he also took advantage of the university's late-night library facilities. Here, he spent time looking in the *Yellow Pages* for manufacturers' contact numbers and then rang them up, picking their brains about the different parts of the process and asking if he could stop by and see for himself.

He soon learned that he had indeed been right, and that the high street opticians were making enormous profit margins on the spectacles they were selling. So he decided to go for it, and set up a website to sell glasses to the public.

His first task was to find some suppliers to make glasses from him. The manufacturers he contacted were mainly helpful and after a few visits, James chose some that he wanted to buy from. But after their initial helpfulness, it proved very difficult for James to persuade them to supply him. Being only 21 and with no business background, most manufacturers were extremely reluctant to open an account with Glasses Direct. It did not help that his whole premise was essentially trying to take business away from the manufacturers' major customers, the high street opticians. Nonetheless, after much hard work and a fair amount of rejection, James found a few manufacturers happy to work with him, and he agreed terms with them.

'It was the moment when he first thought, "this will work."'

As a test, he arranged to forward his own prescription on to the manufacturer, who would then send him a pair of glasses with the correct lenses in. The test worked. When the glasses arrived at his house a few weeks later, at a cost of just £6, it was the moment, he says, when he first thought, 'this will work'.

James planned to focus his new business just on supplying glasses to people with prescriptions, unlike most opticians which carry out eye tests for customers and then supply them with glasses or contact lenses afterwards. He called it Glasses Direct, to make it crystal clear what the business was about, and so that search engines would find it more easily when potential customers searched for glasses or spectacles.

'Most customers spend ages trying on different pairs in opticians' shops.'

There were two major hurdles for customers to buy glasses from a website. The first was needing to get a prescription – people weren't used to getting their eyes tested and walking out of a shop with the prescription without ordering any glasses. Secondly, glasses obviously can make a significant difference to people's image, and most customers spend ages trying on different pairs in opticians' shops. Clearly they can't do that physically when buying from a website. While this is also true for clothes, it is easy for people buying clothes by mail order to send them back if they aren't quite right – but because each pair of glasses is made specially for a customer,

Working from James' home when the company started.

with lenses cut to fit each set of frames, most high street opticians don't let customers simply return them if they don't like the way they look.

James thought about how to get over these issues; if he couldn't, his business wouldn't work. He thought that by offering substantial savings over high street prices, he would be able to persuade enough customers to walk out with their prescriptions and try buying online. He also came up with an idea for a tool on the website which lets customers try the frames on at Glasses Direct using a digital photo of themselves, so they can see what they would look like in each pair before ordering. In fact, this probably works better than the high street shops, since most people can't see themselves properly in a possible new set of frames, not having the appropriate lenses in at that stage. And just to make sure people would feel comfortable buying from the web, James bravely decided to offer a full no quibble refund policy to anyone who wasn't happy with their glasses.

Moving Swiftly

The next step was to design the website. James started developing this himself while he was still studying for his finals at university, and finished it in the summer holidays when a friend who was studying design at university came over to James' parents' house to help him out. James literally went to pick him up from the station and drove him to the house and back day-in-day-out until the website began to take serious shape in early July. The process itself, though hard work, was at least reasonably cheap. As James says, the beauty of an e-business is that one is able to get it up and running quite cheaply; in his case, using the last instalment of his student loan.

All James really needed was his website, and relationships with other suppliers. He managed to get his manufacturers to hold the stock (of frames) for him, and then dispatch the finished glasses directly to the customers, whose addresses Glasses Direct would supply. As a result, James' young company could start doing business without opening its own warehouse or taking on staff. So once this was in place, James concentrated on getting the website ready to go live, after registering the company with the Medicines and Healthcare products Regulatory Agency, which happened on 1st July 2004.

Not surprisingly, given the brand new concept and no publicity, at this stage the website wasn't an immediate success, with sales in the first month averaging one or two pairs a day. But this proved to be the quintessential calm before the storm.

James knew he had to tell people that his new business existed, and that he didn't have a huge marketing budget to do this with. He decided to print some leaflets promoting Glasses Direct, and roped in some friends to help him hand them out to potential customers. He recalls getting on a train at Bristol Temple Meads station and handing out flyers all the way down the train 'so people would have to sit, stuck, with our fliers to read for the whole journey'. It was an advertising manoeuvre that clearly worked: their website statistics showed that many people had logged on to the site when reaching such destinations as Bristol International Airport!

'People were so used to paying £150 for a pair of glasses that they were amazed to see the same deal elsewhere for £15.'

As well as this, word was gradually spreading, boosted by happy customers telling their friends. According to James, people were so used to paying £150 for a pair of glasses that they were amazed to see the same deal elsewhere for £15 – especially the early customers who had placed orders when they were not really sure whether to trust this website or not, and received glasses that were as good as the expensive high street models. Consequently, the rate of orders coming in every day grew rapidly; an average day during August that year saw 100 pairs ordered. Thank-you letters started to arrive too, something that James proudly points to as a real distinguishing feature for his company as compared to the big chains.

Glasses Direct's 'Luke' design for £15.

The offices at Charlton Park, Malmesbury, which the company moved to in late 2004.

He was also lucky, he says, in that his business was very cash flow positive from the early days. Customers would pay by debit or credit card with their order, and Glasses Direct wouldn't need to pay their suppliers until 30 days later, which meant that their bank account grew rapidly with their revenues, which is not normally the case with many startup businesses. In addition to this the young business had very low overheads to start with, another thing in its favour as a startup venture.

Luckily for James, his business continued growing at the same fast pace. After renting some nearby office space within a month of starting the business, he also took on his first 'official' member of staff – someone to manage finances and, as he puts it, 'put us on the straight and narrow' and help get things in order; despite being a web based business, the paperwork from the high volume of orders was enormous, and needed to be filed and monitored properly.

Meanwhile, James was busy trying to drum up publicity for his new business. He wrote to lots of journalists he thought might be interested in the Glasses Direct story, asking them to write about him. In August, the media started to pick up his story, in particular an article in *The Daily Telegraph*. 'This gave the business a massive boost,' James says, as he advises new companies with a 'genuine hook or interesting story' to persevere with getting some strong media coverage; James thinks it's the best way to get a business going.

With such a successful start and great PR, the story sounds like it must have been plain sailing from here on. But it wasn't. James faced significant opposition from the high street competitors and says that this was Glasses Direct's biggest hurdle. He claims that 'the industry hates us,' and he points to a variety of challenges and legal threats to prove his point. However, he goes on to add that in fact the competition has only made the company stronger. The British press love stories of underdogs taking on established corporate giants, and James' personal charm and startling story about the true costs of glasses proved irresistible, leading to lots more high profile articles about Glasses Direct being picked on by the high street opticians. James also admits that these difficulties have only made him stronger, unwilling to stand by and be beaten.

A Happy Ending

In the first 18 months of business, Glasses Direct generated sales of £1.5 million; a tremendous achievement for a new business started by someone straight out of university. James has invested heavily to make sure that Glasses Direct continues to grow; rather than taking money generated from profits out of the business now, every penny made continues to be pumped back into the business, with James intent on all sorts of expansion plans.

James decided to take on outside investors towards the end of 2004, selecting individuals who would provide not only money but also expertise in the optical field. He is keen to build up the company's credibility and provide ever better service to the customer. There is little doubt that having the backing of registered opticians, as the business has now, has strengthened the company's reputation and helped ensure their growth, with turnover figures at the last count hitting £3 million.

'Think global from the beginning.'

With plans for the future revolving around international expansion – with particular focus on the United States – James reveals that Glasses Direct's aim is to sell a million pairs of glasses by 2010. Although confident that this is well within the company's capabilities, James recommends that anyone thinking of starting up a web business should 'think global from the beginning'. To start too focussed on one country and then attempt to expand later only prolongs the inevitable and means you have to play 'catch-up' with the rest of the world when they jump on your bandwagon. James is convinced, with the benefit of hindsight, that if the Glasses Direct website had been launched simultaneously for multiple countries, the company would by now be well on their way to saturating not just the UK market but a global one.

WHERE ARE THEY NOW?

Still working hard to ensure Glasses Direct becomes a household name worldwide, James Murray-Wells has received numerous entrepreneurial awards since starting up the company in 2004, including the UK's most prestigious award for new businesses, Startups.co.uk's NatWest Startup Business of the Year in 2005. The business continues to grow, has had more than two million unique visitors to its website, and has saved the UK public over £15 million on their glasses.

moneysupermarket.com

A Wealth of
Experience

Company:	**Moneysupermarket.com**
Founders:	**Simon Nixon**
Age at start:	**32**
Background:	**Mortgage broker**
Start year:	**1999**
Business:	**Price comparison website**

I n 1999, the UK's first personal finance price comparison site for consumers was launched by mortgage broker Simon Nixon. moneysupermarket.com provided a wealth of information and aimed from the outset to be a 'consumer champion'. It is now visited by more than seven million Britons a month and, although the web has been flooded with replicas, it retains its position as the leading comparison site. Simon began with a solid background in providing accessible mortgage information, which he was able to adapt to his new venture. He was also able to use an existing business model to make moneysupermarket.com's creation relatively painless.

An Entrepreneurial Mind

This extraordinary story starts in 1989 when Simon dropped out of a much-hated Finance and Accountancy degree at Nottingham University in his first year; he had no idea which career path to pursue, much to the distress of his parents. They presented him with the job section in their local newspaper *Chester Chronicle* and 'basically forced' him to apply for the first post he was vaguely suited to, which turned out to be a position as a financial consultant. Simon warmed to the idea of 'making some money', but at only 20, he felt disinclined to sell life insurance and pensions. Following this logic, he decided to specialise in the more relevant area of mortgages. He quickly found that 'the harder you work and the more innovative you are, the more money you make' as he was effectively self-employed, working on a commission only basis.

Simon realised that if he teamed up with a local sales office, he may be able to get sales representatives to contact him directly to set up mortgages for their clients. He approached the nearby Chester Persimmon Homes office and asked if his services would aid their sales, quickly discovering that one in two people wanting to buy homes from them could not as they had been refused mortgages. Simon made himself first port of call for this sales office and started getting five or six mortgage enquiries a day. Soon, having only been working a few months, he was the top sales person in his office. The Managing Director of Persimmon Homes then asked him to provide information for three or four of their other offices. Simon describes how 'all of a sudden, I had someone helping me arrange mortgages'. This experience gave Simon a taste for the success of ingenuity. He also spotted an opportunity: there was no resource in the market for financial advisors like himself to find the best mortgage for their customer.

Realising this, Simon bought an Apple Mac computer and in his spare time put together a fortnightly trade magazine, *Brokers Update*, listing the best deals and every product for reference. He initially sent out 500 free copies and charged £11 per month on standing order, with the first month free. Simon recalls that for every 100 copies he sent out, he received 10 standing orders. It was so successful that within

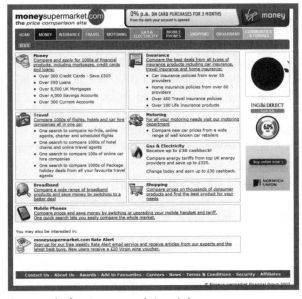

Screen grab of moneysupermarket.com's home page.

three or four months he was making more money from magazine subscription than from arranging mortgages.

Simon recognised he had to focus on either the magazine or mortgage brokering and decided to pursue the magazine as he thought it had more potential and found it more interesting. He recruited two people to work with him, bought a printing press from his savings and leaped into the world of publishing.

The magazine performed well but within two years, subscriptions started to plateau as mortgage brokers began relying more on computer technology. Information could be accessed immediately, so the magazine was already a couple of days out of date by the time it landed on their desk; something had to change. Simon, innovative as always, used funds saved from his magazine and took the format to begin writing a software package that was updated daily over the internet, allowing brokers to enter criteria and find the most competitive mortgage. He was joined by software programmer and business partner Duncan Cameron who, no-longer actively involved, still owns a stake in the company. Mortgage 2000 launched in 1994 and Simon estimates that this software is currently used by about 40% of all mortgage brokers in Britain. He acknowledges that had he just kept the magazine going, it probably would have died a few years later and he emphasises the need to keep 'spotting opportunities' and 'move with the times'.

To house his business initiative, Simon initially rented a room in the Chester Enterprise Centre, where they helped new businesses get on their feet. Eventually he was able to buy a terraced house in the Hoole district of Chester where the company stayed until 1998, when the company purchased its first purpose built office on the then new Chester Business Park, from where they still operate today.

Breakthrough

Simon's 'real break' came in 1999 when Freeserve introduced free access to the internet. He envisaged creating a site that used the information from Mortgage 2000 but changed the interface so that consumers themselves could use it. Simon also decided to broaden the information they could access to include other areas of personal finance including loans and credit cards to create a price comparison site.

Extending research to other areas was easy: with a solid background in mortgages and having produced financial information for several years now, the transition was 'bread and butter to us'. Simon took on more researchers who specialised in personal finance, recruited internet developers and purchased some servers. He feels it is important to have an in-depth knowledge of the business you are dealing in. While some entrepreneurs will jump into a market they think will be lucrative, Simon warns that without sound prior knowledge, there is a greater chance that business will not be successful.

'In business, if you work really hard, you take two steps forward and one step back.'

It was while setting up Mortgage 2000 that Simon went through the hard process of establishing a business from scratch, and not in his second venture - he warns that 'in business, if you work really hard, you take two steps forward and one step back'. Therefore, moneysupermarket.com was able to lean on Mortgage 2000 and benefit from its legal and administrative infrastructure and personnel, of which there were 40 or 50 by this point.

In total, Simon estimates that moneysupermarket.com cost around £100,000 to set up, most of which was spent on PR, and because of Mortgage 2000's success, the new venture already had cash reserves in place. Unlike a lot of internet startups who have to find an investor and 'blow it all on TV advertising', Simon already had a successful business under his belt and had already learnt the principles of being in business. He advises entrepreneurs to follow a 'no frills' policy to setting up.

'People like to shop around and brag to their friend in the pub that they got a bargain.'

When moneysupermarket.com was launched at the end of 1999, Simon felt he had created a truly useful site – the challenge now was to direct internet traffic to visit and use it. Despite having more money in the bank than most startups, there was no million pound fund to facilitate a vigorous TV advertising campaign so Simon and his team had to be more imaginative with their marketing strategy. He notes he was sure people would use the site, as he believes the average UK consumer is 'very price driven'. He explains, 'they like to shop around and be able to tell their friend in the pub that they got a bargain'.

Growing Interest

moneysupermarket.com makes its money every time a consumer clicks on a link to a financial provider such as Barclays or Capital One. So before moneysupermarket.com could make a profit from their site, they needed to set up deals with financial providers and convince them they could provide high quality internet leads. Simon remembers this process was extremely difficult – companies were of course very sceptical, as back then this method of partnership had never been attempted before.

moneysupermarket.com also anticipated that their information might be used by others, sourced through their website. The strategy was to pitch to the big web 'portals', such as BT, Yahoo and Freeserve (who already had lots of readers but relatively 'poor content', according to Simon), and offer them moneysupermarket.com's price comparison tools, splitting any e-commerce revenue 50:50. Simon approached the main players and pitched his novel idea, but was categorically turned down. The companies were not interested in a revenue share and were asking for a fee from him of millions up front, which moneysupermarket.com could not offer. Simon's last appointment in the first week of pitching was to the *Daily Mail*'s financial website, thisismoney.co.uk. They liked the content that moneysupermarket.com were offering so much that they took a gamble and agreed to a revenue share in early 2000.

'Once you have enough inertia behind you, they fall like a pack of cards.'

Simon remembers how after this break, other portals 'sat up' and thought 'hang on a minute, they've got better information than us and they are our competitor'. Once they saw the information in practice, moneysupermarket.com secured the internet portals that had at first declined. Now, approximately 200 portals carry their content.

It also became much easier to set up deals with the financial providers that would provide the income, and Simon describes how the deals slowly 'dripped' in: 'once you have enough inertia behind you, they fall like a pack of cards'. A slow yet rewarding process, within six months (which seems like an age in the internet world) moneysupermarket.com had secured deals with five or six providers and therefore could start producing revenue.

Although moneysupermarket.com did no advertising, Simon did recognise the importance of good press coverage, as this was essential in driving traffic to their site. He recalls they spent nearly £100,000 on PR, using both PR company Lansons, of London, and PR staff employed in-house. Simon ensured his researchers talked to all the national financial press every month – from *The Sunday Times* to the *Daily Star*: financial journalists would obtain figures and statistics from moneysupermarket.com and quote their source in articles. He 'knew straight away that this was one of the most effective ways to drive traffic and raise your profile'. Simon describes this endeavour as a 'little bit cleverer than just spending money on advertising'.

> 'You have to put your foot down on the accelerator or people will catch you up very quickly.'

Although they faced a challenging start, Simon believes this was inevitable as he was pitching a unique idea, essential, he feels, in succeeding. If your idea is not unique, it must at least be a variation of what exists in that market at the time. He believes that if you follow what everyone else is doing, 'how do you stand out?' moneysupermarket.com was the first price comparison tool for consumers in early 2000, and by the end of the same year had been joined by others cashing in on their success. Simon believes that because they were first in the market they had the advantage, but it was crucial they capitalised on this: 'you have to put your foot down on the accelerator or people will catch you up very quickly'.

Moving with the Times

In the first year, moneysupermarket.com made a respectable £500,000 and received around 50-60,000 hits a month. This exceeded expectations, but Simon adds the real surprise lies in their current success, receiving nearly four million visitors to the money and travel websites per month and turning over well in excess of £100 million in 2006. In a way, Simon comments that moneysupermarket.com were 'victims of our own success' as their servers crashed several times to begin with, as they had underestimated the server capacity they would need to cope with the amount of hits they would get. Simon had to quickly adapt their servers to allow for the demand they had generated and he describes the 'steep learning curve' the company went through to rectify the problem.

moneysupermarket.com had one very close call: in 2001, the year of the dotcom boom, London bankers followed lastminute.com's example and advised Simon to float the business, estimating he would get £100 million for it. Obviously intrigued by this estimate (turning over half a million a year), Simon went ahead with the long process of floating the company. However, not long after lastminte.com was floated, their shares crashed and the dotcom boom rapidly turned into a bust. moneysupermarket.com had to pull their floatation four weeks from completion and Simon remembers this was a very painful process that made him a more cautious businessman.

In 2002, Simon and his team developed some clever technology, which Simon admits was groundbreaking then but probably commonplace now. It worked like a 'spider robot': after the consumer keys in their details, the robot searches hundreds of sites and brings back the results on one page, making the site faster, more efficent and fully inclusive in its searches.

Alongside this, the business branched into the insurance market with insuresupermarket.com in February 2003. Successful to the core, Simon proudly quotes that moneysupermarket.com is the largest broker in motor insurance policies, arranging 'something ridiculous' like 850,000 quotes per month. Later the same year, the company launched travelsupermarket.com and burst into the highly competitive travel market. This move may have been a risky one as this was a step out of the financial market they had dominated, yet Simon made sure travelsupermarket.com had something new to offer consumers – their technology ensured they searched every travel provider including, for example, charter flights and aggregators, while existing sites only searched deals from the traditional airlines or agencies. Again, Simon ensured moneysupermarket.com differentiated itself from any competitors as it explored new markets.

WHERE ARE THEY NOW?

Nearly eight years on, the business has grown fantastically. From 2005 to 2006, revenue-earning transactions more than doubled and due to the larger content of the site, page impressions increased threefold. To ensure they continue to increase, Simon Nixon plans new initiatives; the site has recently launched a shopping comparison service.

In 2006, moneysupermarket.com ran its first ever TV advertisement with more advertising campaigns planned for the future. Simon attributed the success of the company to its ability to adapt to changing environments.

The SG Group

Filling the Void with Quality

Company:	Stop Gap - Now the SG Group
Founders:	Claire Owen
Age at start:	30
Background:	Marketing
Start year:	1993
Business:	Marketing recruitment agency

Stopgap (now part of the SG Group) is the UK's leading freelance marketing recruitment agency; in fact the marketing industry credits Stopgap with inventing this specialist area. Its success has been in no small part due to its outstanding treatment of its own staff, which has led to multiple awards for being a great place to work. Today the company has expanded to become the SG Group and has a thriving business in Australia as well as the UK, with revenues of approximately £26m.

A Job Well Done

Claire Owen had worked in marketing for five years before she founded Stopgap. She had also once started a business which had failed; in 1989 after a six month round-the-world trip, courtesy of British Airways Air Miles, she began selling a bizarre, unrelated mix of imported Thai silk and locally painted baskets. A year or so in, she ran into trouble with a supplier and the financial ramifications of any client loss suddenly hit her, so she shut down the business and opted to return to the safer option of permanent employment. Although she was certain that she would like to start her own business again one day, it was important, after her first failed venture, to wait until the right idea came along.

Three years later, in July 1992, Stiletto, the marketing agency Claire had been working at for two years, went into receivership while she was on maternity leave, so she was made redundant. With a four-week-old baby and a large mortgage to pay off, she and her family were facing a world of uncertainty. Claire realised that the client her team had been working for was also left 'up the creek without a paddle', as she describes it. She and her colleagues had been putting together a pan-European marketing promotion for Xerox, one of their biggest clients, and the job was not yet finished.

Claire came up with the idea that she and her fellow account handler, Gaynor Egan, finish the promotion for Xerox, working as freelancers. Having nothing to lose, Xerox accepted her proposal – from their point of view, Claire's team were their only point of contact at the agency, so they would still be receiving the same level of support. Unfazed by the challenge of delivering the work, Claire borrowed a fax, worked from home with her young son under the desk and the promotion was completed a few months later, in September. In essence, Claire had provided herself as a 'stopgap' for Xerox when they were left in the lurch.

Unexploited Potential

She realised there may be a gap in the market for a service providing marketing companies with temporary solutions to their recruitment problems. As she continued to freelance for the next four or five months, she became convinced there was a market

Offices in Richmond: Goodwin House on the right, and Isabella House which they expanded into.

that had yet to be explored. The marketing industry had no specialised recruitment service; in 1993 even the big boys, the Michael Page's of this world, didn't do it'. Other professions had access to temporary staff, such as locum doctors or supply teachers, but in marketing, people used their available friends. This method was far from perfect, and frequently didn't work well, yet at that stage there was no other option.

'Claire could see that she would effectively have this very specialised and sought-after market to herself.'

So Claire approached her contacts and asked if they would be interested in using an agency to provide them with freelance marketing staff, and received a very positive response. In her words, 'they hated recruitment consultants, they were over the moon' at the prospect of dealing with people who understood account handling and marketing language. Claire could see that she would effectively have this very specialised and sought-after market to herself, at least to start with, and decided

The agency team of recruitment consultants and executives at their weekly team meeting.

that this could be the next opportunity that she had been seeking to start her own business.

Early on, she approached Gaynor Egan, the Account Manager of the Xerox account who had also been made redundant, and invited her to become her business partner. While she benefited from having support during the creation of the business, 'which potentially can be quite lonely', Claire now wishes she had considered the impact having a business partner would make in the grander scheme of things: as the business progressed, she felt there was an unequal input of ideas into the company.

Developing the Business Idea

The name Stopgap seemed a logical and explanatory name, encapsulating Claire's idea. Eager to seek advice, she asked her businessman uncle what he thought of the name and he advised her against using it. Obviously, Claire ignored this advice as she felt it a strong name. She urges people to ask others' opinions and 'listen to it, but you don't necessarily need to follow it'. Now, the word 'Stopgap' has become 'synonymous with freelancing in the marketing world'.

'Do one thing, and do it brilliantly.'

Claire did, though, take note of the advice of another businessman she visited with Gaynor in late 1992 to 'sound out our idea with him'. They presented a confusing jumble of business ideas, and he had to ask them to clarify what exactly they were offering. His advice to them was, 'do one thing, and do it brilliantly'. Claire felt this was a 'fantastic piece of advice', and focused their business idea on the essence of Stopgap, which aimed at servicing only a very small area of the recruitment market. She urges others with business ideas to keep their proposition very simple and clear, and to aim to excel at this.

Start-gap

In March 1993, the business was officially launched. It was set up at minimal cost, as, like a lot of service businesses, they did not require any capital investment and in any case they didn't have any money. Confident that their business would succeed without the 'flashy' front of smart cars and grandiose offices, Claire and Gaynor's concern was to provide quality of service. Borrowing some office space, a computer and a phone from friends who ran a design agency, they kept overheads to an absolute minimum. They spent just a few hundred pounds on simple letterheads, business cards and a small advertisement in the marketing press. Claire feels this was 'a great way to start', as she was extremely conscious of finances following her redundancy.

Set Apart

Stopgap set out to be as different as possible from other recruitment agencies and aimed to challenge the industry's reputation for bad service. Claire admits she tried to avoid being called a 'recruitment agency' for as long as possible, labelling Stopgap a 'marketing service', as she was embarrassed to be associated with an industry with a questionable reputation.

Stopgap's approach to recruitment was greatly shaped by Claire's own 'ghastly' experience working with an agency where she felt used by consultants for their personal gain. Because of this, Claire ensured Stopgap created a better experience for both clients and candidates than they were used to; they worked hard on the quality of client and candidate relations from the start. As 'the fundamentals of client service are the same' whatever industry you are in, Claire and Gaynor's skills in marketing and account handling directly translated to the high-quality service they intended to offer both clients and candidates.

'Create your own rules, then you're in charge.'

When setting up, the founders faced the catch-22 situation all recruitment businesses face: do you find the clients or the candidates first? Unaware of any traditional process (neither of the pair had worked in recruitment before and did not know how agencies were run), they searched for both simultaneously. 'It wasn't rocket science', she comments, and believes the business was set up with nothing but common sense. They saw their lack of experience as a definite advantage. Claire's own advice, that she followed while building Stopgap, is to 'create your own

The SG Group's staff (except the team based in Sydney) at an away day held at Center Parcs in the Netherlands in October 2006.

rules, then you're in charge'. Clients were not put off by their lack of recruitment experience – indeed, many were relieved that there was an alternative to standard recruitment agency practice.

The founders endeavoured to create a positive experience for their candidates. Claire was not interested in grades and achievements – she had scraped through her A-levels and still achieved a 2:1 at Bristol Polytechnic University – but focused on understanding a candidate's motivation and aspirations. This, she feels, set Stopgap apart from other agencies who rigidly number-crunched candidates in an impersonal system.

They sourced clients by using their network and sending new business letters to marketing directors. Shortly after Stopgap was established, they secured their first client through one of the introductory letters: Bahlsen, the German biscuit manufacturer needed a German-speaking marketeer and, with a stroke of luck, Claire and Gaynor found and placed a candidate with relative ease. During the first six months, the majority of clients that used Stopgap were companies one or other of the founders already had a relationship with. Claire recalls that they did not have very many clients, probably 20 or 30 by the end of year one, but these clients would use them repeatedly once they had seen the benefits of using temporary account handlers and marketeers.

To find candidates, they placed a very small black and white ad in *Marketing Week* that simply read 'do you want to freelance?' Claire describes how, as 'word got out that there was an alternative way of working', the numbers of candidates on their books gradually rose and 'the career freelancer was born'. She comments that, 'it did amaze me in the early years how the market just grew. Suddenly there was a release of people finding an alternative to permanent work. Stopgap created the opportunity and people came flooding in.' Claire estimates that by the end of year one, they had around 500 people on the books and had fulfilled more than 150 briefs. Keen to keep costs to a minimum, they ran the agency from an Excel spreadsheet. It was two years before this became so inefficient that they created a totally bespoke database.

Claire and Gaynor's approach to payment further differentiated them from other agencies. As Stopgap had had no money when they sent their first candidates to a placement, they asked the client to put them on their company's payroll, and pay Stopgap 15% of the total wage. This meant Stopgap did not have the hassle of calculating charges, which simplified the process enormously. Claire explains that while agencies were charging anything from 20-30%, she, once again, chose to do things differently. In marketing, 15% was traditionally the mark-up price that agencies would charge a client, so, when Stopgap also used it, 'it was a number the marketing world were comfortable with' and one she felt was fair. After nine months, Claire realised that to accommodate clients who had a 'headcount freeze', they needed to set up a Stopgap payroll facility, so she created a simple manual system with the help of 'An idiot's guide to running a payroll' from the Inland Revenue.

In the first year, the company made £60,000 in fees, and the founders paid themselves a modest £10,000 each – their profit was churned straight back into the company. As Stopgap expanded, Claire points out they never had to 'hard sell' the business to clients or candidates. 'There was always a reminder in the marketing press that we were here' but from the beginning up until present day, about 50% of business comes through recommendation and word of mouth.

She emphasises that the expansion of Stopgap only occurred 'when the timing *was* right'. So, when the timing was right, in October 1994, they moved into their own offices in Richmond, and hired their first member of staff. Interestingly, she was also from a marketing background, as was the next consultant who joined the team in January 1996. Claire admits she was keen to avoid hiring recruitment consultants, as they were the antithesis of everything she was trying to achieve. She professes that

The branches of the SG Group, excluding Courtenay.

she continued employing in this vein and as a general rule, Stopgap consultants come out of a marketing background.

As they took on staff, Claire made sure they were looked after and nurtured. After 14 years in recruitment, Claire today obviously stresses that your staff are your most precious commodity, but she does truly believe this. She feels that she has learnt 'you are only as good as the people you employ', and although she knew this at the beginning, the realisation has grown stronger as the years have gone by.

After five years, Gaynor left the business, as her long-term plan was different to the direction Stopgap was heading in. With hindsight, Claire realises that another option would have been to offer Gaynor the chance to join her business venture, but to offer her a profit share without becoming fully-fledged partners.

Claire regrets not writing down the Stopgap ethos earlier. In 1999, while in Australia organising Stopgap's international launch, she was asked to explain the essence behind Stopgap. An Australian colleague advised her to put it in writing, as it will become diluted once the business expands. It was six years into the life of Stopgap before the values they had been working to were written down formally. Claire believes that by being clear about the company's values early on, it will ensure you do not compromise what you are trying to achieve and you will not make the mistake of employing someone who does not fit with your core values.

At the start of Stopgap, Claire admits working in the recruitment industry embarrassed her. Now, her attitude is very different, as she is extremely proud of Stopgap's achievements in the sector they are in. She was also surprised that she found the whole experience of setting up a business very enjoyable. She describes how she loved the thrill of doing something she had not done before and the challenge of attempting new things

WHERE ARE THEY NOW?

Claire Owen continues to be very involved in the business, and has added other divisions including Rightstop, which offers permanent recruitment solutions, Fitzroy, which caters for the upper echelons of the marketing world, and Courtenay, an HR recruitment firm. Stopgap was so successfully established as a temporary service that they needed to create separate brands for the new divisions. These all fall under the umbrella company name, the SG Group.

There are now 127 people working for the SG Group, only three of which come from recruitment backgrounds. The company came 13th in The Sunday Times Best Companies To Work For 2005 *tables and has won numerous other awards.*

Friends Reunited

What Price on Friendship?

Company:	**Friends Reunited**
Founders:	**Steve Pankhurst and Jason Porter**
Age at start:	**Both 37**
Background:	**Freelance software engineer**
Start year:	**2000**
Business:	**Social networking website**

Friends Reunited is the immensely popular website which lets people make contact with old school friends. Founded in 2000 by Steve Pankhurst and Jason Porter following inspiration from Steve's wife Julie, today the site has 18 million registered users, and was sold to ITV in 2005, for a substantial sum.

An Idea in its Infancy

Steve recalls the first glimmer of the idea came in July 1999, when Julie's pregnancy meant that she became very curious as to whether any of her old school friends had children themselves. At the time Steve describes how he had already been considering business ideas for the internet, which was then just starting to take off in the UK, along with his partner, Jason Porter. The two men both worked as freelance software engineers, writing business systems for pension companies. Steve admits he was less than excited about this work, and that he also disliked working for other people and being told what to do and when to do it by. As a result, when he was not working full-time on these systems, he spent his time considering more innovative and web-orientated ideas of his own. As well as toying with Julie's idea of creating a website which allowed you to contact old friends through school listings, he was also considering such ideas as a fantasy football site or a mail-order company which provided party bags for children's parties.

Steve and Julie (pictured with Steve on previous page) – who was also a computer programmer – had always planned that while she was on maternity leave, she could learn how to build a website, and then run one of their ideas as a small part-time business. Consequently, while Steve was working, Julie spent much of her free time surfing the web in order to research her idea for a website which allowed old school friends to re-establish contact. She came across an American website called Classmates which was based on a very similar idea and which appeared to be a success, with five million people registered, even though she felt it was a bit 'clunky and American'. The couple were excited by the existence and success of this website, since it implied that Julie's idea could work well on this side of the Atlantic.

There have been a few jibes that Julie had 'copied' the idea from this American site, but Steve is very clear that Julie's idea very definitely came first and that the existence

'He started to dream Eureka pound signs flashing up.'

of another, similar site, was – and should be – seen as a positive thing. Steve remarks, 'if you have a new idea and nobody's done it, it generally means it won't work'.

Steve says that once Julie had discovered the Classmates website, he started to dream 'Eureka pound signs flashing up'. But while the tingle of that first idea was encouraging, he admits that developing the idea into a business plan was a lot harder than it had first appeared. Julie had recently given birth and the couple soon realised that it just wasn't practical for her to be learning the new skill of developing websites while also getting used to being a new mother. And while they hoped their new website idea might work as a business, Steve also had his reservations, confessing that as he had 'hated' school he had his concerns that it 'would never work'.

And Steve was still working on other website ideas. Luckily, Julie was determined not to miss this opportunity and set to work convincing her husband to build the school friends site. He eventually did, in the summer of 2000, almost a year after the initial idea and as one of several other ideas he and Jason had been floating. Steve and Jason had a list of five or six ideas which they decided to launch on a budget of £7,000 each; they planned to drop them if they seemed to be costing more money than they looked set to bring in.

Steve and Jason raised £50,000 from friends, who received shares in their company in return. With the money behind them they set to work and launched a variety of websites, including an online dating service called Club Event and the party bags project 'Happy Party Bags', an idea that Jason's wife, Anne, had come up with. They were careful not to spend much money and, as they had said they would, canned Club Event after a few months when the £5,000 they had invested did not look set to be returned.

The Launch

Steve began the creative process of setting up Friends Reunited by sending some smiling photos of friends and family to a friend who used the images to make a prototype logo which, incidentally, is the one we still see today. He then registered the domain name after finding that nearly all the names involving the word 'school' had gone and so deciding to opt for a more generic name which reference wider friendship groups. At first they were 'not too happy' with this name and Steve says that it was their intention to find a 'better' name later on but in the end things progressed too quickly.

The website was set up in July, a matter of weeks after Steve had first started building it. They were able to do this very quickly since at this stage their aim was simply to put up a prototype site from which they could gauge demand. Their priority was that the site was simple and fast and didn't ask users for information that wasn't needed. Initially set up as a free service a free service, with the site went live with listings for 22,000 schools from government websites, but no members. Steve recalls that this data entry process was the 'biggest effort' at this stage.

Though free to use for casual users, the men planned to charge people in the future to become a member, when they would be entitled to extra features. They ultimately wanted to get their users to pay for the site rather than trying to fund their business from selling advertising. This made it critical to build up the number of members fast.

'The more people who belong, the more valuable it would become to all members.'

Membership take up however was slow at first; a bit of a concern since the success of the program was reliant on the numbers of members. It was clear to see though that once the site caught on it would be a snowball process whereby the more people who belong, the more valuable it would become to all members. Within the first two weeks, however, Steve remembers receiving an email from one of their members which relayed a successful meeting with a friend he had been at school with 30 years previously; this helped him to realise that the site could really make a difference and stir up strong feelings with people. It was also suggestive of the power of word-of-mouth, and in the absence of a more corporate marketing strategy, which they couldn't afford, Steve used the personal touch to begin getting word out there, through message boards. This involved him posting messages in lots of internet-based forums. Although cheap in terms of marketing budget, it was very 'time-intensive', which was harder to maintain given that he was still working full-time. Although slow to begin with, this method began to pay off and by autumn and Steve recalls that Friends Reunited began to appear on some of the major search engines such as Google, as well as through other message boards as 'a good way of tracking down old friends'.

While Friends Reunited received no money from advertising, they did use a service called 'banner share' as a means of getting the word out; this meant that Friends Reunited would show other companies' banners on its own site, in exchange for those sites showing a Friends Reunited banner on their sites.

This combination of word of mouth recommendations and minimal cost marketing led to the steady growth of the company. In the first two months, membership grew to around 70 users a day, or a couple of hundred a month; by the end of the year they had 3,000 registered members. Steve says that although Friends Reunited was not making much money in those first few months – or, in fact, that year – it did not cost them anything other than a lot of time and energy. 'After all, all we did was provide the core infrastructure, and users generated all the content. We don't have to package or deliver anything. We just support the site,' notes Steve. As a result, of the £50,000 they had raised in startup funds, they found they still had £40,000 remaining. And with both Steve and Jason still working, this really took the pressure off needing to bring in lots of income quickly.

Steve recalls that the first six months after the launch were largely spent scrutinising the site for development and promotional opportunities; gradually adding schools and making sure that he, his wife or Jason and his partner answered every email and enquiry sent their way. They decided to redesign their website in December of that first year, largely in an attempt to make it more simple for the end user – although also, Steve confesses, because the original design was 'awful'! The effect, whether direct or not, was seen in January of the next year.

A screen grab of the site.

Snowball

It was January 2001 before things really began to snowball. The biggest cause of this growth rate was a mention on the Steve Wright radio show that went out on weekday afternoons on Radio 2, with an audience of up to five million listeners. Unbeknown to the FriendsReunited team, the DJ had heard from one of his listeners about the website, and nominated Friends Reunited his 'Website of The Day'. Steve learned of the day's events when the single server they were using to run the website at the time crashed under the weight of 20,000 people who had logged on to search for old school friends. They had to fix this quickly, so Steve and Jason spent the night trying to upgrade the system, which involved adding extra computers in the hope of managing the growing number of people trying to register.

'The website at the time crashed under the weight of 20,000 people who had logged on.'

The site continued to attract media attention and after the site had registered more than 19,000 members, at the beginning of February 2001, it was clear to Steve that they needed to change the way they ran the business away from just a sideline project split between friends. He says that the first real gamble he and Jason decided to take was in quitting their jobs to focus on making Friends Reunited a success, which they did at the start of March 2001.

The second, perhaps more dangerous gamble was deciding to put a charge on the service. According to Steve the site was costing quite a bit by now in IT costs, and profitability was far from certain. As a result, he and Jason reluctantly decided to charge members £5 to make contact with others through the website, whilst never disclosing email addresses. It was, he says, not a figure plucked out of the air but derived from a conversation he and Jason had had in a pub; they knew that the American website charged $25, but felt that a charge of £9.99 was too high. They had just ordered two pints and received very little change from a £5 note, and concluded that £5 was a 'fair amount' to charge for what was an essentially priceless experience, re-establishing contact with a long-lost friend.

They took this decision without doing any market research, but it turned out to be a gamble that paid off. Coming so soon after the initial wave of interest that had been generated by the Steve Wright show meant that profit came quicker than expected. Steve remembers only three people paying on the first day of charging, but these numbers jumped suddenly into the thousands after the first month. The growth continued, and just six months later, Friends Reunited took £1 million in one month for the first time.

> 'They ordered two pints and received little change from a £5 note, and concluded that this was a 'fair amount' to charge.'

Though this was obviously cause for celebration, Steve adds that such fast growth was difficult to manage. By May 2001, the site had hit 'critical mass' so that for the first time, anyone new registering was sure to recognise at least one other name. As a result of this, a few steps were taken to delegate some responsibility outwards – although Steve adds that one of their biggest errors was in fact not delegating enough and trying too hard to 'control everything'. As a result the founders started to become resentful of the experience and the 16-hour days they were having to work.

The founders signed up a PR company to promote the site, hoping that it would free them up to monitor the site's progress, answer emails and conduct interviews. Although the campaign that came about as a result was, Steve says, rather 'reactive', they were able to get their story promoted to a wider audience, which helped the business grow. They were careful to ensure that much was made about the company being a 'bedroom startup in Barnet' and by then, as the dotcom

The outside of the Friends Reunited offices in Oxted, Surrey.

The current four sister sites, derived from Friends Reunited.

bubble was bursting, the company was newsworthy for being 'an internet idea that was successful, without millions invested'.

The growth story has continued since. After overcoming a few hurdles in 2001 – not least the temptation to sell the company (though the offer was for much less than it was worth) – Steve, Jason and Julie oversaw the introduction of a sister service, Genes Reunited whilst membership for Friends Reunited reached eight million people. In 2003 Steve took his own advice and the team delegated managerial responsibilities to a new team headed by ex-*Financial Times* Managing Director, Michael Murphy and have since seen membership continue to grow at an astonishing rate. At the last count, records show that an average of 5,000 new members sign on every day, and the site now has a staggering 16 million members nationwide.

WHERE ARE THEY NOW?

Steve Pankhurst and Jason Porter sold the company to ITV in 2005 for a reported £120million. Since selling the business, Steve has been involved in mentoring for the Prince's Trust and occasionally writes account and booking systems 'to keep the brain ticking over'. His business partner, Jason, is considering becoming a business angel and in the meantime spends his time pursuing his passion for racing Minis.

information in motion

Psion Teklogix

Be in Touch
with Your Market

Company:	**Psion Teklogix**
Founders:	**Dr David Potter CBE**
Age at start:	**37**
Background:	**Academic**
Start year:	**1980**
Business:	**Mobile computer provider for a range of industries. Formerly a software publisher.**

Psion is one of the UK's leading computer companies. Started in 1980 with the growth of the home computer, Psion is best known for its handheld computers, and in particular its Organiser brand which many rate as the best PDA ever made. It also created and later sold off Symbian, the software system which drives millions of mobile phones. Quoted on the London Stock Exchange, today Psion has annual revenues of about £200 million.

Academic Roots

Dr David Potter was born in South Africa in 1943. He has deep academic roots, having taught theory in applied physics at Imperial College, London and University of California at Los Angeles (UCLA); in fact, he taught theoretical physics at universities in the UK and US throughout the 1970s. While doing his doctorate, he began using large mainframe computers, which cost millions at that time, to study simulations. Through this, he became knowledgeable about computer work – indeed, while he was at UCLA, the microchip was invented, and so David was close to this burgeoning area of technology, and began to consider what it could lead to.

'I set up Psion because I believed the chip would drive a new economic revolution in the world. I wanted to be a part of it. It's a bit like being an artist in 1870 during the Renaissance – you wanted to be in Paris, you didn't want to be in, say, Stockholm,' says David.

It was obvious to me that the chip's emergence was going to change everything. Against the cautionary advice of my colleagues I resigned my academic position. They thought I was completely mad because it just wasn't done to do something like that, particularly for academics,' he adds.

'They thought I was completely mad because it just wasn't done to do something like that, particularly for academics.'

So he decided to set up his own business, initially on a very small scale indeed. He didn't have a grand business plan but carefully studied what was then a very tiny industry. There was Apple, Acorn and a small set of adventurers, but that was about it. Back then the entire industry was only worth $3 billion, whereas today it is probably

Sienna, one of the products sold by Psion.

worth $3 trillion. A lot of the technology was coming out of the defence world, but there was a hobbyist element too, where people didn't really know what to do with it. It was clear to David that there was soon going to be massive changes.

He wanted to earn a decent living, but other than that didn't set Psion up to earn vast amounts of money: 'I did it because I thought it was going to change people's lives,' he comments. 'Also, because it was new, there were plenty of opportunities for me.'

David was one of the earliest people to realise that you could make good money from software. 'There were a lot of people on the side that developed bits of software for these tiny microcomputers. I thought that I could market and distribute them in a way that was larger and more professional than they could do themselves,' he explains.

Going it Alone

So he set up Psion, to be a software publishing house, in 1980. Why the name Psion? 'I wanted a name which was short, strange, unique and sounded hi-tech,' recalls David. In the first year it was just him. His first task was to find some software to publish; he managed to persuade some software people to let him publish and distribute their software, which he did by advertising in magazines. Then David got them to tidy their products up so any flaws and bugs were ironed out.

This software was on cassettes that people ran in an audiotape machine wired up to their computer – this was before floppy disks were widely implemented. David made up exciting and inventive names for the products and designed professional packaging for them – a far cry from teaching theoretical physics!

David knew he needed to promote his software, so he advertised in various computer magazines that began to appear around this time. Which, combined with advance payments to software writers and the costs of the packaging, meant that Psion's startup costs were not insubstantial.

David was fortunate in being able to fund the company entirely on his own at this stage from profits he'd made investing in small company shares: 'When I returned to England as an academic, I thought about how I could earn a proper salary on the side. I researched small companies very carefully, invested large chunks into them and made a lot of money. That formed the capital I needed to start Psion. These investments were also an extremely good training ground as to how businesses operate,' he remembers.

Then he approached Acorn and Sinclair (another UK company which had started to do particularly well with 'home computers' at this stage) and their distributors and negotiated deals with the distributors, and sometimes the principal hardware sellers, to distribute his software with their products.

> '*I was identifying the channel to market and I did that well – the volumes shot up.*'

'By doing this, I was identifying the channel to market and I did that well – the volumes shot up,' notes David. This made it easier to sign up other software developers – 'more and more software writers approached me, wanting me to distribute their products.'

Series 5, one of the first hand held computers.

He learnt a lot about the market in that first year. And Psion turned over £120,000, made a profit and even paid him a salary – not bad for its first year in business. But was David satisfied? 'Yes. The first year was setting up the base and I achieved that. More important than the turnover and profit I generated, I established how to reach the market. Once I did that, I was then able to bring in development people without high risk because I was operating a turnover and gross profit.'

Creating a Team

Then, David employed his first member of staff, Dr Charles Davies, someone who'd done his doctorate under him and who was very skilled in software. The company started making its own software, and progressively, Psion started to employ its own development people – including ex-students and colleagues of David's, who were highly-skilled people and were happy to join the exciting young business. By its second year, the company had about 20 people pumping out programmes that David would then define in market terms: 'My staff would come to me with half-sketched ideas, which I would then evolve and define.'

Many of their products proved to be superb. 'We created one of the world's first flight simulators – we worked out how it was seen through the eyes of the pilots, how the plane flew and the aerodynamics of it. We sold millions of that product,' David remembers, with understandable pride.

'They really captured people's imagination.'

There was more serious stuff too, such as spreadsheet and database programmes, but it was games that really sold in large volumes – 'they really captured people's imagination,' explains David. Psion started producing more and more games, such as Hungry Horace, Chequered Flag and Horace Goes Skiing. They were producing early versions of the games which have since grown into an enormous industry that is now larger than Hollywood. 'We pioneered a lot of that, which was terrific and great fun.'

David created funny names for the products so that people would look at them twice, which worked well (a strange twist on the Japanese games which ended up with funny names due to translation errors, for example the game which should have been called Monkey Kong ended up being called Donkey Kong, which became a cult classic). We got a much greater reach and volume through the hardware distributors and manufacturers like Acorn and Sinclair, which ended up buying copies of some Psion products to give away with every new computer they sold, which was terrific business for Psion.

'We always insisted on our own brand being on the product which went out with their computers, which was a good way to market ourselves. We were getting terrific leverage, and we built the brand,' David explains. From the second year Psion took on a PR agent to give advice, but most of it, especially in the first year, David did himself.

Taking Off

In the second year, the company turned over £1.6 million and made pre-tax profits of £620,000, which was highly impressive, especially for a company with a capital base of just £60,000. This financial achievement was considerably beyond David's expectations: 'I never thought when I started that I would make that amount in the second year on a small capital base.' Amazingly, in the following year they doubled the turnover again to £3.2 million, and made £1.6 million profit. 'I think we became number one in the home microcomputer market in 1983, when we were selling with Sinclair and Acorn,' David recalls.

As the company grew, its name was increasingly getting around, and many people came to David for jobs. He was able to hire those who were of high quality in the software side and then, eventually, in the hardware side. By the third year they had about 50 staff. They understandably had very highly skilled people because of the academic background. However, David remembers a character called Steve Kelly who became a very famous games designer in his own right:

'He wrote me a rather sad letter saying that he was 19 years old and unemployed. He said that he had taught himself how to program Sinclair machines and included a written out program in the letter. He was ill-educated and unemployed but a very gifted character. I said to him he should come down to London to see me and that I'd pay his travel expenses. He ended up joining us. He was a very gifted games designer and was very driven.'

> '*It's the customer who hires and fires us and gives us the profits or doesn't.*'

David believes passionately in being in touch with your market. 'If you want a golden rule, that's it: look at the market and listen to the customer. Ultimately, in business, it's not the shareholder who is key, it's the customer. We didn't intend to go into games, but the market led us there,' he reveals, before adding: 'It's the customer who hires and fires us and gives us the profits or doesn't. You should have antennae twitching like the ears of the deer, always looking for what the customer wants and how you serve them.'

Psion was working in a very small industry to start with, but grew steadily, and started developing handheld computers. David felt that although Psion had done very well from computer games, the games industry was becoming increasingly like the pop music industry, with games' shelf-lives falling fast. He also felt that his organisation was slightly more serious in culture, and that there were plenty of opportunities elsewhere. So he explored alternatives, and felt that a handheld device to organise people's increasingly complex lives would be successful. At that stage there really was no such thing as a handheld computer, and the word 'PDA' hadn't been invented. At this stage, David observed, many companies were starting to have one computer to an office – and David felt that there was potential for a smaller device to be used by everyone.

When Psion launched the world's first handheld computer, the Organiser, as early as June 1984, it made it onto the *10 O'Clock News* on ITV! It was utterly revolutionary, using technology never seen before in consumer products. It was about that time that people began to say that something was going on in the industry. Four years on, computing was becoming big news, as David had known it would.

Psion grew each year for 20 years – to do this it had to evolve in a fast-paced market. The number of companies that came and went in the IT industry was extraordinary. 'A business plan should change as you get market feedback; you should be thinking along the lines of "let's suppose it's not working – how will we respond?"' David advises.

WHERE ARE THEY NOW?

David Potter remains an active Chairman at Psion, and has been awarded the CBE. Psion continues to thrive at the cutting edge of handheld computing devices, though it now focuses on business and industrial, rather than consumer, applications. It merged its key enterprise business in 2000 with Teklogix, a Canadian business. The operational business is now named Psion Teklogix.

One Small Step
One Giant Leap

Leaping into a Niche Market

Company:	**One Small Step One Giant Leap**
Founders:	**Nick Schwefel**
Age at start:	**40**
Background:	**Retail Director at Monsoon**
Start year:	**2002**
Business:	**Children's shoe retailer**

One Small Step One Giant Leap is something different in the world of children's shoes. Founder Nick Schwefel wanted to differentiate his company through its aim to make the shopping experience as pleasant as possible, and the rapidly growing chain of stores reflect this. The shoe shops boast a modern theme, better ranges than their competitors, and ample numbers of well-trained staff. Parents have unsurprisingly been won over by the stores, and the company has won Children's Footwear Retailer of the Year two years running. Nick's plans for One Small Step to get big quickly seem to be well on track.

Impressive Grounding

Nick was Retail Director of international fashion chain Monsoon by the time he left to start his own venture, something which is even more impressive considering his first job in the company was that of a van driver. He worked his way up via head office positions in IT, operations and merchandising. In particular, in 1992 he was made responsible for a loss-making five store division of Monsoon called Accessorize; he managed this as it grew into the immensely successful high street staple it is today.

This remarkable journey, during which Monsoon had grown from a tiny unknown company to a high-profile business with around 280 stores, gave Nick a retail background second to none, as he gained thorough experience in almost every area of retail. Along with his natural affinity for the retail industry, this grounding was to stand him in extremely good stead when he set up One Small Step One Giant Leap.

While still at Monsoon, Nick saw the attractions of owning a fast growing, successful retailer, and began to be approached by investors interested in backing him to start something new. In 2001, he left Monsoon, and began to think seriously about the right retail business to start.

'It became clear that everyone had similarly poor experiences with shopping for their children's shoes.'

He spent around three months looking at various retail concepts and exploring ideas. One of these was children's shoes. Nick and his partner had two small children, and had experienced first hand how frustrating shopping for their shoes was. Talking to other friends with children, it became clear that everyone had similarly poor experiences with shopping for their children's shoes.

The main problems were poor service, principally caused by long queues (often over an hour) and frequently shops not having the right size of shoe in stock after a long wait. Most stores' ranges were also small, and the environments frequently very tired.

It struck Nick that this was probably the last area of 'needs retailing' to be modernised: children's shoes are not an option, parents simply need to buy them. Yet the shops selling this necessary product were predominantly dated, and featured none of modern retailing's benefits. His experiences of it left him with the impression it was a poorly performing area and he knew he could do what it took to fix it. He rightly believed that if he could solve the problems he identified within the sector, he would be able to build a solid business.

'Children's shoes are not an option, parents simply need to buy them.'

Luckily, one of the investors who had approached him while he was at Monsoon, thought that Nick's idea could make a great business, and agreed to finance the early stages.

The exterior of OSSOGL's store in East Sheen, London.

Preparing to Jump

As with everyone who thinks they have discovered a great new idea, Nick spent some time thinking about why no one else had set out to build a specialist chain. One likely explanation is that the business opportunity is far from easy. You need to buy stock long in advance, and each shop needs lots of stock – there is a wide range of sizes of each item, including different width fittings for many shoes. On top of this high cash cost to open, then, the profit margins available aren't great – nothing like as high as fashion or accessories, for example. And staff need quite a bit of training to be able to measure children's feet properly and to fit shoes well. 'All in all, it's a very hard one to get right,' Nick explains.

Getting it right was something he was intent on doing though, and he didn't waste any time. After making the decision to go into children's shoes, Nick set the business up properly in August 2002, with a clear plan to grow to at least 40 stores. However, it would be a while before the first shop could open – first, Nick needed to hire a buyer, then order the stock, which takes months to arrive after being ordered, at the same time as finding the right site for the first shops, and developing a brand look and feel.

Some of the girls' shoes range.

Nick did extensive research with people in the children's shoe industry to try to find a really good buyer, since he knew how important this would be. In particular he needed a buyer who had extensive experience in the children's shoes area: Nick knew how to run a retail business, but was new to the area of children's shoes. He managed to find someone who was buying children's shoes for another retailer, whose family worked in the children's shoe industry, and who already felt that there was scope for a really well designed specialist children's shoe retailer. She joined, and gave the business a real boost.

He decided to start the business with one town centre store and one 'local' store, closer to where the target customers lived, and see which worked better. After considering lots of possible sites and bidding on quite a few, Nick eventually found two sites he liked for the test, one in the centre of Bath and the other in Sheen, West London. He persuaded the landlords to accept him as a tenant – not straightforward for a new business, especially for the more prominent store in Bath. In the end paying a rent deposit helped convince them (most established retailers would not need to pay rent deposits) and the first shop opened in May 2002.

Nick spent a long time planning the look and feel of the stores. Many children's shoe shops feature bright colours in their logo, appealing to the younger children; Nick chose not to go down that route, preferring a more neutral, fashionable look which would not turn off the older children as they get more fashion aware.

The first stores were very successful. They were bright, spacious and airy, as Nick had planned, and they were both on the ground floor – something Nick realised mattered after he noticed customers with prams or buggies having difficulties in stores retailing out of basements or first floors.

Nick says now that, 'in retrospect the shops were probably slightly too large and expensive, we probably should have gone for a smaller format to start off with,' but, as he explains, working out what premises suit a new retail offer is a tricky business and is something that gets easier as the business grows and can compare different approaches.

The Giant Leap

Nick's plan was to roll out a large number of successful outlets relatively quickly as soon as he had established the best model store. This meant that as it became obvious that the Sheen store was the best performer out of the initial two, Nick was able to use the comparison to the Bath store to refine his business model, so One Small Step now started to concentrate on opening local outlets in affluent areas, rather than high street stores in provincial towns.

'One Small Step started with a warehouse, a proper retail IT system, an office and a small but experienced team.'

The infrastructure put in place at the beginning of the company's days clearly shows a business model focused on expansion. Not for Nick was the traditional startup situation of a one-man band operating out of a front room. Instead One Small

The neutral and contemporary shop interior.

Step started with a warehouse, a proper retail IT system, an office and a small but experienced team.

Nick explains: 'We knew we wanted to expand the business, and we knew we wouldn't be able to expand past two shops if we were just doing it from our front room. So we had to make sure we would be able to expand in future years and not spend our whole time moving premises or trying to fit new IT systems while running a dozen shops; I know from my past experience just how hard it is to grow a business at the same time as trying to put in new systems – as well as how important those systems are to understanding what is really going on in a retail business.'

The benefits of this strategy were invaluable in 2006, which saw the opening of eight more stores. The company was able to take this expansion in its stride and hardly change a thing regarding the company's infrastructure. The forward-thinking business plan has meant that turnover has been able to increase massively with relatively little upheaval.

However, getting the business to this stage has not been cheap. Opening each new store is an expensive process, with refurbishment and stock to pay for as well as the rent, and in the early years the business has had to fund its warehouse and back office team.

Investment in One Small Step has primarily come from business angels, although the company has also seen received investment from a venture capitalist – in one round of funding in 2004 the company received £1 million, £250,000 of which was from venture capitalist YFM, and £750,000 of which came from private investors.

Bringing a venture capitalist on board was a big change for One Small Step, which had been working until then with just the original investor. The company had to start to work with far more formality and had to introduce a formal board of directors, something which has taken a while to adapt to but which has proved beneficial to the company.

'It's not a concept that would make massive amounts of profit in six months.'

Finding business angels to invest in One Small Step has been relatively easy from the start, and has got easier as the business has grown. The fact that the concept of the business is straightforward and easy to understand helped it gain investors in the early stages, but the difficulty has been with the fact that such a business is relatively slow to build. As Nick says, it's not a concept that would make massive amounts of profit in six months: sales at each store, he explains, take several years to reach maturity, when the stores generate full profits.

Nick is not overly equity-precious, but, along with the original investor, he has retained control of the business. 'There's always going to be an equity sacrifice for whoever invests at the beginning. It's better to have a smaller piece of a bigger pie than a big piece of a small pie,' he laughs.

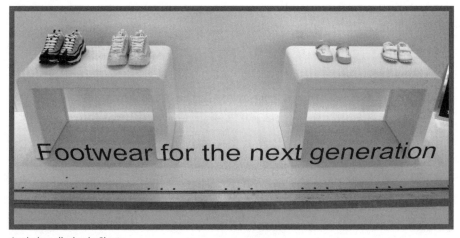

A window display in Sheen.

Raising money has been a constant issue for the company, but the biggest challenge for the business came in the initial stages of starting up, when the two brand new shops had to be filled with stock.

Nick explains that the children's shoe industry is 'very protective'. It proved extremely difficult to get brands to agree to be sold in the new stores, especially the sports brands. He spent incredible amounts of time and effort selling his business to suppliers in order to get the stores the ranges they needed. This was a key stage for the business, as one of its unique selling points was the range of brands it stocked compared to its competitors. Nick succeeded, though, and managed to get the brands in early enough to achieve the range he wanted. However, it took around 18 months to open an account with one major sports shoe brand.

Inevitably Nick found himself being very hands-on in the early stages of the business. He cheerfully admits that being responsible for the accounting before the company hired a bookkeeper was a particular challenge! Since then Nick has been able to install tiers of management throughout.

Nick talks about the importance of a good business plan, coupled with the need to be flexible enough to adapt away from it. 'Business plans are essential for working out how much money you will need; the difficulty about business plans is that it's hard to predict the future of where a business is going to go from a very small set of information,' he says. 'A business model that doesn't surprise you is very rare.'

Nick admits that there would be a lot of things he would do differently if he were to start up all over again, but he philosophically notes that this is all an inevitable part of the learning process. 'You're learning all the time. If you don't learn from your successes and failures then you just don't move on.'

WHERE ARE THEY NOW?

Nick Schwefel remains at the helm of the business and today One Small Step employs eight people working in the head office, as well as about 90 people working in the shops.

In a relatively difficult time for retail the chain continues to grow and One Small Step is certainly moving upwards. In a marked contrast to the early days, brands are now desperate to get their products stocked in the stores, which if nothing else, proves that the company is progressing not with small steps, but with giant leaps.

JoJo Maman Bébé
maternity | baby and child | nursery and toys

JoJo Maman Bébé

Convalescent
Inspiration

Company:	**JoJo Maman Bébé**
Founder:	**Laura Tenison**
Age at start:	**25**
Background:	**Clothes making and property development**
Start year:	**1992**
Business:	**Maternity and baby clothes retailer**

It's not often that car accidents can take credit for inspiring new businesses, but a particularly bad smash which left Laura Tenison badly hurt ended up doing just that. Now the business she built afterwards, a mail order and retail business supplying pregnancyware and children's clothing, has won awards, grown to have high street presence all round the UK, and made a fortune for the ambitious and determined Laura.

Finding and Funding Her Passion

According to Laura, her entrepreneurial skills were sharpened from a young age, even making dolls clothes in exchange for pocket money aged eight. She remembers always being keen to run her own business, and acquired her own sewing machine by the time she was 13 to take orders for made-to-measure wedding dresses. Later she did an 18-month apprenticeship at Aquascutum, then went on to make and sell haute couture men's clothing. So she was clearly a natural fit for the rag trade, and aged 22 she was determined to launch her own clothing business.

But while the skills and the self-belief were there, Tension had no capital to set up a new clothing business. As a result, aged just 22, she decided to get into the property market in France with the view, ultimately, to building up a good business which she could sell to fund the clothing manufacturing company she dreamed of. Despite having no experience in property, Laura had noticed a gap in the market on a trip to France: selling, renovating and letting houses in France to British clients. She felt that she would be able to channel her French language skills and the experience she'd had doing up her own flat in London into filling that gap. The lucrative property market, furthermore, was, she says 'a good way in' to starting a clothing line as it had low startup costs and overheads. She could thus afford to start the property company with just £2,000, borrowed from one of her brothers, which was handy as the high street banks turned down her request for a loan.

After travelling round rural France to find suitable properties to let, Laura would find British clients by putting advertisements in the UK press. She ran this business for three years and sold it in 1992. The sale of this business raised about £70,000

Laura with her two sons.

for Laura, who then persuaded a bank to match it with a £70,000 loan with the view at last to setting up a clothing manufacturing company. Although Laura knew she wanted to set up some sort of clothing company she says that she was still at this time unsure as to what area she would be focusing in on, and was indeed quite open to ideas.

The Birth of JoJo

The idea which became JoJo Maman Bébé came to her in a remarkable way. At Easter-time in 1992, Laura was involved in such a bad car accident in France that she was flown by air ambulance back to the UK with two broken legs, crushed ribs, a shattered foot and damage to her cheeks and jaw, confined to hospital for a long rehabilitation process thereafter. Because the orthopaedic ward she was due to stay on had no beds, Laura recounts how she was transferred to a cancer ward shortly after her arrival. It was here that she met the woman with whom she credits as providing the inspiration for JoJo Maman Bébé, 'the one stop shop for all your maternity, baby and nursery needs'.

According to Laura, sometime during her recovery – when she was 'compus mentis again' - she got talking to the woman in the bed beside her and discovered that this woman, who was 32, was a mother to two young girls who she wished to purchase some clothes for. She was upset, Laura recalls, because while she was too ill to leave hospital, she could not find anything she considered nice in any of the mail order catalogues, complaining to Laura that what was available was often limited and of a poor quality.

'She recognised that this lady's comments might be just the fantastic business opportunity she was looking for.'

Although Laura had no experience in the childrenswear market and was not a mother herself, she recognised that this lady's comments might be just the fantastic business opportunity she was looking for. As a result, she describes how she plotted an early release from hospital, and once out – despite still being in a wheelchair – started work immediately.

The shop front in Cheltenham.

The first thing she did was look into whether the complaints raised by her hospital neighbour were experienced by other young mothers. Was this really a gap in the market? She concluded, of course, that there was a gap, and she set out to fill it.

Laura printed 10,000 questionnaires and used a mailing list of people interested in childrenswear for her research – which she says now was far too many (300 might be a more sensible number!). This research taught Laura several key points about her chosen market. Firstly, she noted that while people did certainly want nice childrenswear, what they predominantly wanted was maternity wear because, she says, 'there was nothing nice and fashionable at that time'. She also found that as well as there being a definite gap in the market, the timing looked to be spot on- in 1992 Britain was experiencing something of a 'baby boom', whilst the economy was in deep recession. Laura found that many career mums who were being made redundant were finding this an opportune time to have a family and not return to work, thus the birth rate was 'flying'.

After conducting this research, Laura acted fast and drew up some designs for clothing she thought would be appropriate. She then set to work seeking to find another company to do the manufacturing, and hired two part-time employees who could assist her with taking orders, modelling the samples, overseeing their warehouse and eventually, dispatching orders.

According to Tension, she decided to sell the clothing via mail-order, as, she says, she wanted the company to become 'as mass market as possible' and maternity wear was already itself something of a niche market, with approximately 500,000 women a year falling pregnant.

The name for the company came from her desire to find a brand name that was appropriate for both adult and children's clothing. 'JoJo' was chosen as a unisex baby name and 'Maman Bébé', french for mother and baby, derives from her time spent in France and her love of the country. From this amalgamation, the rather poetic JoJo Maman Bébé was born.

JoJo's Cheltenham interior.

Teething Problems

After putting her collection together, Laura then turned her attention to finding suppliers. This, she says, was where she encountered her first real problem; for although she had had some experience licensing haute couture clothing which, as made-to-measure pieces, could be produced on a smaller scale, she found that the mass-market was a different story. Factories in China required minimum orders of 2,000 units per style, while factories in Europe needed 3,500. Laura knew that starting a new business was risky, and wanted to keep the risk to a minimum, and so wanted to make just 50 units per style initially, hoping, ultimately, to grow JoJo Maman Bébé to mass-market levels. Because of her ambitions, she wished to avoid using small manufacturers, who, she says, tended to charge too much anyway, which would hurt her ability to make a profit.

It was while doing the rounds at a trade fair in Paris that Laura, who has always been committed to ethical trading, found the answer to this problem by way of a delegation from Columbia. To promote non-drugs trade, the EEC had recently suspended import tax on Columbian produce for a short period, meaning of course, that the cost of importation to Britain would be cheaper. When Laura approached the representatives to enquire as to how much they would charge to produce 50 of a given design, she found the prices they offered her were reasonable.

Some of the designs were more complex than others, needing more labour to make. Initially, Laura decided to produce these pieces which featured more complicated designs (and which she did not want to commission large quantities of) using the Columbian supplier, whilst also making 'bits and pieces' in France. Although it was not a long-term solution, since Laura confesses that she ultimately wanted to manufacture in Europe, this was an excellent way to get started, enabling her to produce small quantities of early designs cost effectively.

'Anyone launching a mail order company is required to put absolutely everything into catalogue production.'

The other step that Laura obviously had to take when launching her mail order business, was to create a catalogue. This was of the utmost importance, she points out, as anyone launching a mail order company is required to put 'absolutely everything into catalogue production' in the hope that you are going to secure sales from it – not only is it a huge financial investment for any mail order business, it also determines whether or not the business will succeed. Consequently, after the collection was designed and made, models – ex-professionals who were friends of friends – were cast and the layout was decided. The actual graphic design element was outsourced to a friend who ran a graphic design company conveniently located in the office which they shared. Later, this friend's company did not work out as intended and the friend ultimately came to work at JoJo Maman Bébé full-time.

'You should never let the fact that you're inexperienced get in your way. If you don't know how to do it, ask people and work it out for yourself.'

Next, Laura set to work compiling a mailing list, starting with the names that she had gathered whilst conducting her market research. She then wrote a press release – despite having had no previous experience – by copying the format from a friend who worked in a press office. According to Laura, this is the way one must always play it – you should never let the fact that you're inexperienced get in your way. In her own words, 'if you don't know how to do it, ask people and work it out for yourself.'

First Steps

In this case, the timing was just right, with JoJo Maman Bébé making its way quickly into the press, which Laura attributes to the fact that there were very few 'fashionable' maternity wear collections around at that time and that what JoJo Maman Bébé was doing was exciting and new. Laura recalls in particular, such innovative early ideas as making a maternity version of the black business suit. In those days, she says, companies designing maternity wear tended to produce frumpy clothing such as tent dresses and dungarees and would always avoid black due to 'mad superstitions' that wearing black might somehow cause you to miscarry. But when Laura commissioned such items she found that various niche groups picked it up and that people responded well; as a result she says that part of creating a successful business is sticking your neck out and not being afraid to try something new.

'Other companies tended to produce frumpy clothing such as tent dresses and dungarees and would always avoid black due to mad superstitions.'

It is a plan that has enjoyed much success. In JoJo Maman Bébé's first year it sent out 30,000 catalogues and sold clothes worth £50,000, a figure which increased five-fold in the following year to £250,000. It has not, however, always been plain sailing; 18 months into JoJo Maman Bébé's lifespan, the pound devalued by 10% causing all of Laura's purchases, made primarily abroad, to become more expensive. Because the profit margin at this time was less than that, Laura was left in a situation where she had to raise more capital than she had already. The banks, she remembers, would not look at her, having already matched the £70,000 she had put up at start of the previous year. As a result, Laura re-mortgaged her house, as she was convinced of the success of the company – which she believes had the sales but was just underfinanced. While Laura ultimately made the money back, she admits that mortgaging her house was, of course, not part of the original plan and as a result she warns those who are starting their own business to always have a contingency allowance to cover the costs if a disaster should ever strike.

Despite such problems, faith in the company has certainly paid off. Since its second year, JoJo Maman Bébé has continued to grow at an average yearly pace of 25%, far exceeding Laura's initial expectations of a growth rate of 10-15% a year. She suggests that part of the reason for their success was the fact that she put her business plan into action quickly at a time when the market was relatively untapped and there was a definite demand for her product. She does, however, point out that since that time the market has become 'saturated' with competitors and there is now a large variety of both good and bad maternity wear. This, she says, has meant that JoJo Maman Bébé has had to be 'very good' in order to survive.

The recent nautical boy's fashion range.

Laura recommends, firstly, taking educated risks when you know you can afford them, a key example of her own being the decision to move into retail in 2004. While this was itself a risk, Laura describes how by building up a database of nearly a million customers, she was able to ascertain where the main buyers were located and concentrate store locations in nearby 'local' shopping areas that customers could access easily. Laura also suggests a focus on the negative rather than positive aspects of the business as a means of ensuring high standards. By having the grit to focus in on problem areas in your business and not back away until they're solved, she says, you will, ultimately, help to ensure the future of your company.

WHERE ARE THEY NOW?

Laura Tenison is still heavily involved with JoJo Maman Bébé, owning 99.5% of the company's shares and overseeing the majority of all decisions made. The company has successfully launched high street shops and a website from which customers can buy its goods. It currently has about 15 stores nationwide, with more opening regularly. Sales from the website have proved invaluable – making up as much as 48% of the total orders. The company's recent accolades include being named the Retail and Leisure Business of the Year at the Fast Growth Business Awards 2007 where Laura herself was named Female Entrepreneur of the Year.

BRAVISSIMO

Bravissimo

A Personal Solution for a Large Market

Company:	**Bravissimo**
Founders:	**Sarah Tremellen**
Age at start:	**28**
Background:	**TV/radio marketing**
Start year:	**1995**
Business:	**Lingerie, swimwear and clothing retailer**

ike many great new business ideas, Sarah Tremellen's Bravissimo began life as a solution to a problem. When Sarah fell pregnant in 1993 she discovered there was a shortage of attractive lingerie for women whose bust size was larger than a D-cup; this very personal story has clearly had much public resonance as over a million women have contacted the business since Bravissimo was launched in 1995. By 2007 the company had a turnover in excess of £29 million; a growth which has been steady since its earliest years, and has made Bravissimo one of the UK's fastest growing companies.

Solving a Big Problem

According to Sarah, who went up six bust cup sizes during her pregnancy, the idea for Bravissimo was first conceived during a discussion with a friend who had also experienced difficulties buying larger sized bras. They realised that their plight was not unusual and yet the high street failed to offer women like them an attractive range of lingerie in any one place. As Sarah explains, high-street stockists have to offer a variety of styles to their customer and so they tend to stock this large range of styles only in cup sizes A-D to suit their assumed customer-type, and are therefore only able to stock two or three 'big cup styles' to suit customers with a larger bust.

'An awkward thing for to do for many women...
and the experience had been demoralising.'

This situation meant that large-busted women would enter a shop and see a range of bras they couldn't fit into and so would often have to ask the shop assistants which styles were available in their size; an awkward thing for to do for many women and meant that even if the bra they eventually left the store with was wonderful, the experience of buying it had been nonetheless 'demoralising'.

Sarah understood this and her aim therefore, was to create a lingerie mail-order company which specialised in larger bust sizes, where 'everything was provided under one roof', and at the same time to create a 'forum' where big-breasted women could not only feel comfortable with their figures but could celebrate their size.

Sarah's first idea was to open a shop in the vein of those she thought so conspicuously absent on the high-street. But she soon realised that she could not afford to purchase the amount of stock she would need to fill a shop and it became clear that a mail-order business would suit her financial restrictions better since she

The outside of Bravissimo's flagship store in Margaret Street, off Regent Street, opened in November 2006.

would only need to place orders for goods once customers had ordered from her. This quickly became a more viable option as Sarah realised she could also start the mail order business from home, which was also a convenient starting place for a new mother.

At the start of her pregnancy Sarah and her husband had organised their finances to account for the fact that Sarah would not be working, in order that she would become a full-time mum, and therefore there would be only one income coming in. As a result of this planning, Sarah was able to spend a reasonable amount of time investigating her business idea – a key stage in setting up a new business – without the pressure of having to earn a living.

Sarah set about her initial research by enquiring in high street stores, writing to fashion magazines and reading market research reports in libraries. Whilst doing this she also discovered that there was a government scheme which offered a £60 weekly enterprise allowance to people starting up new businesses, in exchange for compulsory attendance at a weekly evening business course which would run for eight weeks. Knowing that the money would come in handy and that the information could be valuable, Sarah signed up almost immediately, merging her small allowance into her standard account and spending her time learning about key startup issues such as how to register for VAT and self-employed income tax. At the end of the course each student was expected to show what they had learnt, presenting a business plan to the head of the course. Sarah excelled in this, using it as a chance to offer a prototype of her product. At the end of her presentation a bank manger, who happened to be sitting on the panel for her course's presentations, told her that she really liked the idea – and offered her a £10,000 loan on the proviso that Sarah and her friend, who was now to become her business partner, invested £3,000 each. They accepted, and the business was established.

At the time, Sarah's husband was working for Tetley Tea as a planning manager and he sensibly informed her that in order to run a mail order company she would, need a database. Admitting that it 'hadn't even occurred' to her, she accepted his offer to write one for her – despite his lack of experience in the field.

As it turns out, it was a wise move. After three months labouring over the computer system a primitive version was ready; and a more complete one followed a few months later that was used for the next seven years. Tailor-made to suit exactly Bravissimo's needs, Sarah recalls it was a wonderful thing as if she wanted the system to do something different she had only to ask her husband to make the amendments. The only downside, she adds, was that the company became dependent on one person. Today, it has an IT department!

Forced to Think Laterally

This was just the beginning, and the journey ahead was by no means smooth. It was at this early stage, while the company was still being set up, that Sarah ran into her first major problem.

'They had enough influence to convince the manufacturers that supplying Bravissimo would be a bad idea.'

Just four miles down the road another mail order company – which also had a shop – was already in operation, and was buying bras from the same manufacturers that Sarah and her partner had begun to approach. Despite the fact that Bravissimo were at that time only a mail order company, the other company objected to Sarah's business setting up in such close proximity and decided to contact many of the large bra manufacturers to try and dissuade them from supplying Bravissimo. This company was a well-established brand and therefore they had enough influence to convince the manufacturers that supplying Bravissimo would be a bad idea.

Only a few days before the other business began to intervene, Sarah had been to a trade show in Birmingham and had approached several manufacturers who she says had been 'really positive'. However a few days following this show these manufactures started to contact Sarah to withdraw their support. Sarah later found out this was a direct result of the other business contacting the manufacturers and persuading them that supplying Bravissimo would affect their established business relationship. Sarah points out that the bra manufacturer's sales representatives worked on commission and so were keener to continue to deal with a secure, established brand rather than risk

Sarah with an early range of bras.

dealing with her, a brand new business with no experience in the sector.

Sarah recalls that it was at this point she became 'really determined', citing this 'horrendous' experience coupled with her first-time experience of motherhood as the fuel which spurred her on. Echoing the mantra of self-belief so necessary for those starting up a business, she describes how this convinced her for 'the first time ever' to stick with something and to make a success of all her hard work.

At first Sarah tried 'begging and pleading' with the manufacturers, only to be told that they absolutely would not supply her. Resolute, Sarah reconsidered her approach and remembered an article she had read at her university careers centre which suggested that many people who rang up companies asking for a job were immediately told 'no', but those that rang up asking for advice were often able to be seen and consequently might 'get through the door'. So with this in mind, Sarah decided that she would approach the manufactures simply to 'talk' to them about their market. By doing so she was able to retain contact with them whilst she considered what other options were open to her.

Sarah briefly considered the idea of manufacturing her own bras but says this was never really what she wanted to do. 'We weren't bra designers, we wanted to deal with the public', she says. It was in Autumn 1994 that she decided instead to devise what she refers to as a 'cheesy marketing document' to persuade manufacturers that

Interior of the Margaret Street flagship store. (Courtesy of The Nest)

they were making a big mistake in not supplying Bravissimo – that if they did not supply Bravissimo they would be missing a fantastic opportunity.

This 'cheesy marketing document' turned out to be one of the best things to happen to the new business, forcing Sarah 'to think about what her business was really about' and ultimately lead to the creation of Bravissimo as a more wholly marketed brand which celebrated the full-bodied figure. During this marketing planning process, Sarah came up with the idea of producing a 'magazine' which exceeded the scope of traditional bra catalogues by including articles and letters about similarly large-busted women.

Sarah outsourced the design of the magazine to a friend of a friend who was just starting up herself and therefore offered them a 'cheap deal'. Once the outline of this was in place, Sarah approached Honor Blackman – who was also a friend of a friend – to feature in the magazine; something she was 'only too happy to do'. Sarah points out that there often seems to be a common desire amongst the famous to 'champion the underdog' and it is therefore worth approaching such people through any tenuous link.

'I want people to shop with us, because they want to shop with us, not because we stop them shopping elsewhere.'

And so it became this combination of articles, features and photos in its mail order catalogue that set Bravissimo apart as a brand and ended up its saving grace. The idea went down so well that the three manufacturers Sarah showed it to all agreed to supply Bravissimo. In addition they agreed to supply promotional pictures of the merchandise for the first published magazine – saving Sarah money on production costs. Sarah's dream was starting to come to life.

While her primary aim had been to convince manufacturers that Bravissimo was an opportunity not to be missed, Sarah still had to overcome the problem of the rival company. This she did by creating the perception that Bravissimo was an Oxford based company, and was no longer in London, since the problem their competitor had was their location in the near vicinity. Sarah decided to create a 'virtual office' at her parents' house in Oxford, to where she set up a PO Box and an Oxford telephone number which was on permanent divert to London. She was very careful never to let on publicly that Bravissimo were not an Oxford-based company. As part of this she would drive to Oxford twice a week to collect items – a extreme measure, but according to Sarah, all this was necessary as a means of allowing the company to focus on making itself a positive brand rather than the victim of a competitor's negative campaign. This focus is still important to her and has since been incorporated into her business practice, as she states, 'I want people to shop with us, whatever the competition, because they want to shop with us, not because we stop them shopping elsewhere.'

The rival company eventually discovered, via a mutual contact, that Bravissimo was still based in London. However, by this time their attempts to thwart Sarah's efforts were unsuccessful. Sarah had by now produced the magazine and was buying stock from the manufacturers who now had faith in Bravissimo succeeding. The competitor's attempts to rid themselves of Bravissimo's competition only resulted in their increasing unpopularity and four years later this rival company disbanded after expanding too quickly and running into cashflow problems. In a suitable twist of fate, Sarah managed to buy their mailorder list from the receivers; as she says, 'so often in life, what goes around, comes around'.

Displays in the Margaret Street flagship store.

A Magic 24 Hours

Having won support from three bra manufacturers and with a finished magazine, Sarah was finally in a position to launch Bravissimo. This she did in January 1995. Now, looking back, she admits that at this time she was naïve and inexperienced and working with only 'a bit of common sense and gut feeling'.

Together with a few friends and her husband, she created a database with just 75 people as target customers. These names were a combination of friends, family and people she had encountered when conducting her research or attending trade shows. Sarah explains that one major benefit of starting with such a small base was that it allowed her to 'evolve, develop and learn' without making mistakes that impacted the business negatively. While most businesses have to rely on other people's expertise, she says she was able to 'take time and work on a trial and error basis' and so deepen her understanding of the business.

Three days after sending out the first catalogue and magazine, Bravissimo made its first sale – albeit from Sarah's business partner's mother-in-law! Over the next three weeks approximately 150 people registered on the mailing list and around 30 bras were sold. However after three weeks Sarah had an 'enormous dose of luck' which would get really get Bravissimo off the ground.

As part of her 'launch plan' for the business Sarah had sent a number of the first 5,000 copies of Bravissimo's magazine to various newspapers and women's magazines such as *Good Housekeeping* and *She*. It struck a chord with a journalist from *Femail*, the women's section of the *The Daily Mail*, and the result was a double-page spread in a Wednesday edition of the newspaper. This feature led to an explosion of interest and in the three days following the article, Bravissimo received a staggering 1,500 calls. This surge continued for some time so that by the end of that first year, there were 11,000 women registered on the database and Bravissimo had sold £134,000 of underwear.

Sarah and her business partner hired their first member of staff in the summer of 1995 and another before December of that year, along with some temps to assist with the administrative work – one of whom is still there 11 years on and is today Bravissimo's Product Director. Sarah explains that the people she hired were often not particularly interested in the fashion business, but she had difficulty recruiting those who were, since they were not interested in working with two women, new to the industry, who were working from a sitting room! Furthermore, as the company continued to grow at a pace (turnover for the second year was £400,000) there was little time for a long, formal recruitment process and help was often taken where offered. With hindsight, Sarah now warns of the importance of adequate delegation, saying that as the company grew during its second year so many people were hired to do relatively menial tasks that they became something of an 'amorphous mass'. Eventually Sarah and her business partner decided instead to train people to do specific jobs and delegate responsibilities accordingly. Over the last 11 years Sarah has granted more and more of her own responsibilities to the 380-strong team which now surrounds her.

'It didn't bother me that I wasn't being paid – although if it had gone on for 11 years, then I might not have been so content!'

Although Bravissimo's turnover has grown steadily since its launch (currently in excess of £29 million), the business did not make a profit until the summer of 1998. By this time Sarah had bought her partner out of the business. Unusually, the lack of profits early on did not cause problems due to the nature of the company's positive cashflow; as a mail-order company Bravissimo bought goods from suppliers once it had received orders from customers. The customers paid up front, but Bravissimo had arranged six week terms with its suppliers so Sarah could use new customers' cash to pay for last month's goods. This meant that even though on paper Bravissimo was not making a profit, there was always money in the bank and the company was able to break even in cash terms for the first three years without having to take out any outside loans.

Sarah was not phased by not seeing any profit in the early years. She says that her focus was elsewhere, 'I loved the idea of setting up a business because I loved creating something and developing it and watching it growing bigger. It didn't bother me that I wasn't being paid – although if it had gone on for 11 years, then I might not have been so content!'

WHERE ARE THEY NOW?

Sarah Tremellen is still very much involved with Bravissimo today. After running the business under her sole ownership for three and a half years following the departure of her partner, she was joined by her husband six years ago. They now run the company together.

In 1999 Bravissimo opened its first high street store, and has since gone from strength to strength. At the time of writing there are 13 stores open across the UK with plans to open more. A website shop has been opened now selling the full range and Bravissimo has also moved into to selling swimwear and clothing for larger busted women.

THE CINNAMON CLUB

The Cinnamon Club

The Rocky Road
to a Good Curry

Company:	**The Cinnamon Club**
Founders:	**Iqbal Wahhab**
Age at start:	**35**
Background:	**Journalism and PR**
Start year:	**2001**
Business:	**New style Indian restaurant**

I n 1998 Iqbal Wahhab had a vision for a new type of Indian restaurant. He saw how popular Indian food had become and yet that none had made the quality leaps so evident in modern British and European restaurants. He aimed to prove that an Indian restaurant could succeed with chic, modern décor and haute cuisine – and ultimately to win the first Michelin Star for an Indian restaurant. The Cinnamon Club, which he opened in 2001, broke the mould in Indian cooking and is now one of London's hottest dining experiences. The restaurant's path to success was difficult, and the subject of a BBC *Trouble At The Top* programme, but in the end the restaurant Iqbal had originally envisioned did open and is now established as one of London's top restaurants.

Discontent With Tradition

Previously, Iqbal had worked in and around the Indian restaurant business. In 1991, he founded a restaurant PR business and worked with a variety of eateries, including several of the then top Indian restaurants and Michelin starred French restaurants. The different attitudes that Iqbal encountered in each establishment led him to consider untapped potential in the Indian restaurant market. He had identified a number of ways in which service, décor and food could be improved. He felt that in Indian food, flavours got lost in the sloppy curries soaked up with copious amounts of naan bread, and helped down with lashings of beer, whereas French cuisine produced crisp, delicate flavours. He also had hang-ups concerning the service at most Indian restaurants, which he found to be infuriatingly poor.

In 1994 Iqbal founded the Indian restaurant trade magazine *Tandoori*, to create a forum for his sponsor, Cobra Beer, to communicate with Indian restaurants in an informative way. He made a spectacular exit from this magazine when he harshly criticised the way Indian restaurants have traditionally been run, with flock wallpaper, stained menus and poor service. So condemnatory were his words that he received a plethora of complaints and even a number of death threats from disgruntled Indian restaurant owners and waiters – and had to leave the magazine and go into hiding for a spell. With hindsight he believes that his comments were 'ill-judged'.

Suddenly unemployed, Iqbal was driven to personally change the way Indian cuisine was viewed and the idea for the Cinnamon Club began. With no prior knowledge of restaurant management, a background of journalism and PR and a degree in politics from the London School of Economics, he aimed to 'see how far our imagination would let us go when it came to redesigning and redefining Indian food'. He had attempted to influence change from afar, now it was time for him to get his hands dirty.

The Dream

Iqbal saw an opportunity to take Indian cooking one step further. In his opinion, Indian food was stuck in a rut and needed new energy and, well, spice. His vision was twofold: to completely redesign the presentation of Indian food and to fundamentally change the way in which the food was cooked. Ultimately, Indian food was to become wonderfully presented in a more delicate, more European style. Relying on gut instinct and blind determination, there was no way of knowing whether enough people would actually want this cuisine to make it a commercial success, though the sheer growth in popularity of Indian food suggested that there should be enough demand to make the restaurant viable.

A New Process

Iqbal's admiration for French cooking was paramount in the creation of the Cinnamon Club's dishes. He intended to take a European design template and re-construct Indian food within it. He appointed Eric Chavot, a two Michelin-starred French chef, as consultant to his management team early on, and soon poached two managers from famous London restaurants The Ivy and Le Caprice. In his quest for staff, he then ventured overseas.

Iqbal met Vineet Bhatia, an ambitious chef from The Star of India in South Kensington who shared his passion for creating a new style of Indian food. Next, the new venture needed money – as much as £1 million, needed to convert premises, build dedicated kitchens, fit out the restaurant to a high standard, stock up with wine, recruit and train staff, and promote the new restaurant.

Iqbal turned to friends, family, contacts, and

An artist's impression of what the restaurant would look like after renovation.

business angels – people who invest in small, private companies in return for shares in the business. He pitched to a network of business angels, serving potential investors a variety of delicious items to eat to demonstrate the sort of cooking The Cinnamon Club was to feature. He found some of the money needed, but not quite all.

At this stage the path became rather more troublesome. Without all the money, Iqbal wasn't able to sign a lease on the premises he had targeted, a prominent position on High Street Kensington. Someone else was, and the premises went off the market. But worse was to come.

Vineet was ambitious, and became fed up with the delays. He left the venture to become chef at Zaika, which went on to become the first Indian restaurant in the UK to win a Michelin Star. In addition to this, one of the investors became unhappy with the slow progress, and was threatening to sue for his money back. The fledgling venture urgently needed a top new chef, a new site, and some additional investment.

A scouting mission and a friend's wedding led Iqbal to Vivek Singh, the head chef at the Rajvilas, Rajastan's most exclusive boutique hotel. There they experienced a 'meeting of minds' and Singh was offered the job on the spot. Iqbal, Vivek and Eric toured India in search of inspiration using every available source, from five star restaurants to Bombay street food.

The completed restaurant interior.

They returned to London and began work on creating a new style of Indian cooking. Iqbal insisted his chefs understood the basics of how a French kitchen works in order to apply these principles to Indian cuisine. Based on French reduction techniques, the team layered spices within each dish so that a delicacy of flavours was created. The Cinnamon Club believes this technique is a unique style of Indian cooking and therefore sets it apart from all other Indian cuisine. Spices sourced by Iqbal and Vivek from all regions of India were (and continue to be) air freighted fortnightly to England in order to get the freshest, most authentic flavours possible.

'*For the first time ever, wine became the main drink served at an Indian restaurant.*'

The more delicate style of layering spices also made wine a better accompaniment. So, for the first time ever, wine became the main drink served at an Indian restaurant, as befits The Cinnamon Club's fine dining experience.

Restaurant Novice

Through an agent, Iqbal eventually found another potential site for his restaurant – the Old Westminster Library. Two private viewings with other bidders had already been set up, and it seemed doubtful The Cinnamon Club would get a look in. Assertive as ever, Iqbal gatecrashed one of the viewings and felt the 12,000 square foot old library's character and charm would perfectly compliment his cuisine. However, as he did not have an appointment, the landlord's agents refused to deal with him. Following this, he 'pestered' the landlord's office continually until he secured a meeting. Amazingly, after Iqbal had presented his proposal, the landlord decided to go ahead with The Cinnamon Club.

By now, the project had consumed even more money than planned, and the new venue needed more money to bring it to life. Iqbal calculated that his venture now needed £1.7 million. It is here where he experienced major problems and with no restaurant experience, was on a steep learning curve. Inevitably this affected the running of the project - he admits that at the start, in common with many entrepreneurs, he could not even read a balance sheet. He encourages budding entrepreneurs to make contingency plans, to expect things to go wrong and even plan them to: 'ask those really awkward questions right up front, don't leave it until later on'.

They had to be people who loved dining out. If it were people who loved numbers, they wouldn't have been interested.'

Financing the project became a year-long task. Encouragingly, a bank manager aptly named Paul Cinnamon endorsed £1 million through loans and overdrafts. Still, he needed to gather private financiers willing to invest. While Iqbal could view his lack of restaurant experience as a positive, enabling him to strive for a higher vision, potential investors usually wanted more experience. Iqbal relied heavily on his vision to inspire investors who wanted something tangible for their money. As he says, 'they had to be people who loved dining out. If it were people who loved numbers, they wouldn't have been interested'. At the time, The Ivy and Le Caprice had just sold for huge amounts of money, demonstrating that investing in fine restaurants could be profitable. Even so, Iqbal had to be very persuasive.

The capital was raised eventually through a very successful banker at Morgan Stanley who loved the concept so much that he invested the maximum amount possible under the Enterprise Investment Scheme and persuaded colleagues at

Morgan Stanley, Merrill Lynch and ICAP to do the same. Finally, the process of creating an upmarket Indian restaurant in the Old Westminster Library could begin. This grade II listed building added to the grandeur of the dining experience and set it miles apart from high street Indian restaurants. The project ran out of funds seven times due to unforeseen structural problems and the renovation work needed on such an old building. Budget over-runs are common when embarking on such a large-scale project and Iqbal had to approach his investors for another £800,000, making the grand total needed £2.5 million – well over double his initial estimates.

The Private Dining Room on the ground floor of the Cinnamon Club.

The Cinnamon Club's exterior on Great Smith Street, London.

'He soon realised that he was more than the promoter of the business: he was the manager.'

With the benefit of hindsight Iqbal acknowledges he was too focused on PR, which was his 'natural tendency'. He soon realised that he was more than the promoter of the business: he was the manager and was accountable to his board of investors and shareholders for the finances and proper running of the company.

The founder admits he was often left clueless after meetings with architects, mechanical engineers and quantity surveyors. His lack of experience made him heavily reliant on his management team and often unsure of his own role.

Nethertheless, in April 2001, the restaurant opened with a lavish launch party, which lots of press and celebrities attended. The party was a success, and The Cinnamon Club was finally open. Even the angry investor from the early years was satisfied – Iqbal met him for lunch, and offered to buy him out. The food and premises were so good, though, that the investor preferred to stay on.

Even the restaurant's opening, though, went far from smoothly. Gas and electricity had not yet been installed, as it hadn't occurred to Iqbal that it was his responsibility to order it. So the launch party food was cooked using gas canisters to power the kitchen.

Having learnt the hard way, Iqbal encourages others to have a thorough knowledge of how your management team works. What was originally expected to be a nine-month project ended up taking two years. Managerial naivety literally cost Iqbal big-time.

At first, Iqbal's eagerness for large-scale media coverage backfired when some early reviews were not favourable. Some critics argued that the Old Westminster Library was too grand an environment for Indian food while others found the food itself pretentious: its chefs were accused of 'messing' with Britain's favourite food. The management was accused of only being concerned with Michelin stars, rather than customer satisfaction.

> 'He had seen a niche in the market which customers were not yet aware they wanted filling.'

So despite sales of over £2 million in its first year, the restaurant performed considerably worse than expected. The management team responded to the initial critics by fine tuning their product, and urging people to not be so quick to judge. Iqbal describes going on a 'charm offensive' to woo the public and critics back. By the end of the second year, sales had grown considerably. Iqbal emphasises that it was imperative for people to understand what the Cinnamon Club was trying to accomplish in order to appreciate it; he had seen a niche in the market which customers were not yet aware they wanted filling.

Ultimately, The Cinnamon Club succeeded because Iqbal's vision was right, and the management team's restaurant experience and skills were able to deliver it.

WHERE ARE THEY NOW?

Today, The Cinnamon Club remains a thriving restaurant, winning consistent praise from customers and critics alike. Its sales have grown steadily, and hit approximately £5 million in 2006. Leading London restaurant guide Harden's now describes it as' London's best-known Indian'.

Iqbal Wahhab left The Cinnamon Club in 2005. He founded British restaurant Roast in 2005, in London's trendy Borough Market, where he was able to learn from some of his mistakes. His focus has been less on PR and more on pleasing the customers in the first instance. And according to Iqbal, it's working.

S&A Foods

Spicing Up
Supermarket Shelves

Company:	**S&A Foods**
Founders:	**Perween Warsi**
Age at start:	**30**
Background:	**Full time mother and housewife**
Start year:	**1986**
Business:	**Ethnic food manufacturer**

S&A Foods is not a name known by most people in the UK; yet millions buy their products every day. The company makes high quality ready meals for supermarkets, who market them under their own brand. Started by Perween Warsi 20 years ago, the company has been a resounding success, and now employs 750 staff and has a turnover of more than £75 million.

A Bland Market

Perween Warsi was born in India in 1956 and moved to the UK in 1975. She had two children with husband Talib, a family doctor, and could have quite easily remained in what she describes as the 'easy life' of mother and housewife. However, Perween says that she always had a desire to 'stand on her own two feet' and, after her sons were of an age where they needed their mother less, she began to look for something else to do. She was particularly keen to run her own business and was on the look out for the right venture to set up and run.

Her 'eureka' moment arrived in one of the most ordinary places – a supermarket. It was 1986 and Indian food was becoming part of the mainstream with supermarkets trying to sell pre-cooked curries – the foods that British consumers were increasingly buying at takeaways. Perween noticed for the first time that samosas were on sale and, her curiosity raised, she decided to buy some. However, when she tried them, she was horrified, stunned that food of such a low quality was available for sale in a major supermarket.

Her response, however, is what sets her apart from the masses of other people who would have bought the 'sub-standard' food that she ate that day – Perween vowed to make her own food and to begin a business selling it.

'I tried some so-called Indian foods and I was quite appalled by them and I thought "I could do a far better job".'

'I tried some so-called Indian foods and I was quite appalled by them and I thought "I could do a far better job",' she said. 'I thought that people were ready to eat Indian food and that they deserved to eat something better, something delicious.'

Cooking Up A Plan

Perween spent some time mulling over her idea and deciding on her next steps. She decided that she needed to conduct some 'market research' and embarked on a simple yet highly effective strategy. She prepared some samosas in her own kitchen and took them to a local Indian takeaway to see if they would sell. The owner took them on and the food turned out to be a success. Pleased with her small victory she moved on to the next logical step and started providing the shop with a regular supply. The quantities of food and the money raised at this stage was very small, 'six samosas for £2.50', Perween recalls gleefully, but the most important fact was that people liked them.

From these humble beginnings she began to seek other buyers and approached other takeaways and delicatessens in her local area to try her food. She also expanded her product range to begin to sell tandoori chicken, pakora and other finger foods. A cook all her life, Perween was able to recreate in her kitchen at home the foods that she had made and eaten as a child in India. Although she admits that she had never encountered an onion bhaji, so she had to learn how to make one – just one more part of the learning curve.

One of S&A Foods' most popular oriental dishes, beef in black bean sauce.

Perween decided that the market research had worked – that she could make a better product, and that people would indeed buy it, as she had expected. So she decided to start building a proper business. She named the company S&A Foods, after her two sons Sadiq and Abid, and was up and running quite quickly, supplying a range of finger foods to a number of stores. She wanted to supply the major supermarkets with her food, but knew that she would need to build up a proper business before it was worth contacting them – they wouldn't be able to give her a contract to produce huge quantities of food until she was at least a little more established than one woman working out of her home.

Later the same year, knowing that she wanted her business to grow, Perween began sourcing ingredients from trade suppliers rather than retail shops, which brought her costs down considerably. She recalls trawling through suppliers in order to hunt down the ingredients at the best price. Perween carried on selling her products herself, calling on potential shops to try to persuade them to buy, and delivering the food to her growing range of customers. She also did all the bookkeeping, sending out invoices to customers and ensuring that they paid them, so that she could then in turn pay her suppliers. She was supported throughout by her husband, Talib, who helped her when he wasn't working at his GP practice.

It was hard work and, as most people find when starting up their own business, Perween found that she had a great deal to learn. She found herself working an exhausting 16-18 hours per day, however she is a tough character and was determined to succeed.

Soon Perween took on her first staff to help prepare and cook the food, still based in her kitchen at home. Within a few months, as the business continued to grow, she had a team of five women working in her kitchen, which freed Perween up to get out and carry on the other essential tasks of making her business work.

'*I never took my eye off my real plan, which was to sell to major retailers.*'

S&A Foods, while still very much a small business, was making money and while this would have been enough for some people, Perween had set her sights far higher. 'I never took my eye off my real plan, which was to sell to major retailers,' she says.

The Taste of Success

Perween began making calls to supermarket buyers, phoning up the head offices and asking who the right person would be, and then trying to get through to them on the phone. Initially, she just wanted to find one that would 'give her a try', but success didn't come instantly. Supermarkets are notoriously hard for new companies to break into, especially businesses with no staff who have never had any relationships with them before. This is not some sort of supermarket bias against smaller businesses, but simply the natural result of a competitive market – lots of businesses want to persuade these buyers to stock their products, so the buyers end up with hundreds of people constantly trying to make contact with them. Perween confirms that you need to be very persistent in order to break through and get your foot in the door. She was armed with extraordinary belief in herself and her food, and believed that it was just a matter of time.

Later in 1986, the persistence paid off and Asda made contact with her. They invited S&A Foods to supply sample foods for a blind tasting session they were organising to test different possible new food options. Perween's foods would be up against established food manufacturers, and a group of people would vote on which food they thought was the best. The tasters would be unaware of who had made the food and would simply make their decisions on taste alone – the ultimate test of S&A's products.

'They told her that S&A's foods had been voted the best in their category and that the supermarket wanted to place an order with her.'

Perween still vividly remembers the day Asda rang her with the results. They told her that S&A's foods had been voted the best in their category and that the supermarket wanted to place an order with her. She was delighted and felt that her hard work and belief in herself had finally paid off. However, there was one small problem. The supermarket was under the impression that Perween was the owner of a well-established business that would be able to meet the hard demands of an aggressive buyer charged with meeting the needs of hungry UK consumers. In fact, at this stage her fledgeling business still operated out of a kitchen in her house. Perween wondered

S&A Foods began with producing Indian cuisine, for example prawn masala.

what to do about this. Should she attempt to struggle her way through and quickly set up a factory in order to meet the incoming orders, or should she own up and admit that she was simply not ready to meet a nationwide demand?

'It was a testing time as I had to decide, do I go and tell them the truth and say "look I have this business but it's not a manufacturing business" or just keep quiet and set up a factory and start producing from it? I always believe that in any long term business relationship there has to be transparency and honesty – so I decided to take that chance and live with the consequences' recalls Perween.

She called the buyer and told her that S&A Foods was a recent startup and that she was not ready to meet a huge order that day. There was a fair measure of 'shock' on the part of the buyer who could hardly believe such a small business was the producer of products that had beaten the opposition so convincingly. However, Perween had both shown strong passion and initiative in applying while still a small business, and also had created foods from her own recipes that were better than any other on offer.

'*I realised that the British people were ready to eat Indian food and supermarkets were ready to buy it.*'

By playing it straight with the supermarket, it had bought Perween some time and confidence while they thought about what they wanted to do. Perween began to get her business in shape for the next stage in its development. After discussing it with her husband they decided to use their savings to invest in the business. It was

Outside of S&A reception in Derby.

a huge personal risk, as all young companies are, but it was also one which was calculated. Perween had done her research and knew that there was a buyer, a market and that her products were good. She says, 'I realised that the British people were ready to eat Indian food and supermarkets were ready to buy it.' But she still had one question she couldn't know the answer to: could she really deliver the quality of food she wanted in the larger volumes the supermarket needed?

Perween found some premises on an industrial estate in Derby which she expected she could renovate to suit her needs. Far from being a food preparation unit, it was a former car-valet depot, and would need substantial work before it could be used to prepare food. She decided to take it on, and signed a lease. She had the interior tiled and installed all the other fittings and equipment she needed to turn the industrial unit into a kitchen suitable for large-scale production.

Perween remembers how tough it was in those early days, as she was completely new to the whole concept of food production. She had not anticipated the stringent demands placed on her by the supermarkets with regards to issues of food safety and hygiene. There were hurdles to overcome but she stuck to her course and, one by one, got over them. (Perween admits that food safety standards set by the supermarkets are far tougher today than during the 1980s, when she started). With determination, her savings and a lot of hard work, she was able to bring the unit fully up to speed within a few months, and production began late in 1986.

S&A began to supply Asda and Safeway followed suit shortly after in 1987 with the same method of introducing S&A Foods' products into their blind tastings, and from this winning the contract. At last, Perween had accomplished her dream of providing major supermarkets with her own good quality Indian food.

S&A's journey to the top was by no means easy and the company had to make a number of tough financial decisions before they got there. In 1988, S&A joined the Hughes Food Group which allowed the company to invest in a purpose built factory, on a Greenfield site in Derby and led to the creation of over 100 jobs in the area. During this time, S&A Foods grew from supplying finger foods to the retailers, to, in 1989, supplying Indian ready meals. Joining with the Hughes Food Group allowed the company to do this quicker, and on a much larger scale. Perween now feels it was a good decision to join, as primarily it allowed for the investments to be made.

In 1990, the company also launched the 'Shahi' brand and, when the opportunity arose in November 1991, Perween and her husband bought back the business from Hughes Food Group, in a management buy out with the help of venture capitalists 3i, bringing S&A Foods once again came back under her control.

WHERE ARE THEY NOW?

In the 20 years since she founded S&A Foods, Perween Warsi has become one of the UK's most admired and well-known female entrepreneurs. She was awarded an MBE in 1997 and was recognised again by the Queen in her jubilee's honours list in 2002 with a CBE.

S&A Foods grew steadily during the 1990s and built another, larger factory next door. It has added a range of frozen and chilled foods, diversifying its offering from the original finger foods, famously gaining the patronage of TV chef Ken Hom. By 2004, Perween had regained 100% control of the company, and is still the owner of the business today. Today S&A Foods is believed to have sales revenues in excess of £100 million and sells its products internationally.

Other books by David Lester include:

STARTING YOUR OWN BUSINESS

THE GOOD, THE BAD AND THE UNEXPECTED

This book reveals what it is really like to start your own business and explains how you can make it happen. *Starting Your Own Business: The Good, The Bad and The Unexpected* is the only book of its kind that combines comprehensive practical guidance with extensive and informal real life examples.

Written by an entrepreneur who has started several successful businesses, this book addresses the questions and fears you may have about starting your own business. And it shares a huge wealth of information, experience and advice while remaining an informal and enjoyable read.

STARTING YOUR OWN BUSINESS

THE
GOOD

THE
BAD

AND THE
UNEXPECTED

What it is really like and how to make it happen
DAVID LESTER | FOUNDER OF STARTUPS.CO.UK

Author: David Lester
ISBN: 978-1-95458-401-4

If you liked this book, you may also enjoy:

BUSINESS NIGHTMARES

Rachel Elnaugh

Rachel Elnaugh, brought to fame as a Dragon in the BBC show *Dragons' Den*, speaks about her fall from grace and the high-profile collapse of her market leading business, Red Letter Days.

In *Business Nightmares* she recalls her darkest hour, persuades successful business personalities, including **Jeffery Archer**, **Doug Richards** and **Gerald Ratner** to open up about their own troubled times and how they faced the dawn…

Author: Rachel Elnaugh
ISBN: 978-1-85458-409-0

A book to make your business stand out:

BRIGHT MARKETING

WHY SHOULD PEOPLE BOTHER TO BUY FROM YOU?

Why should people bother to buy from you when they can buy from the competition?

Bright Marketing reveals that in a world of mediocrity it only takes 5% difference to stand out from the crowd. This revolutionary book shows you how you can apply simple, practical changes to your business to ensure its success.

Written by industry expert Robert Craven, MD of the Directors' Centre, this book is based on the results of his work helping thousands of companies find their edge and improve their profitability.

Author: Robert Craven
ISBN: 978-1-85458-404-5

ABOUT STARTUPS.CO.UK

Startups.co.uk is the UK's largest and most popular online resource for people starting their own business. It has more than 10,000 pages of independently written, practical advice and information designed to guide you through every step of starting up.

From formulating an idea, to writing a business plan, raising finance, finding suppliers and reaching customers, you'll find everything you need to make your first key decisions as a business owner.

In addition, we have more than 50 'How to start...' guides detailing every aspect of starting up an array of different businesses – from qualifications you'll need to the cost of equipment and rent. Whether you're looking to become an eBay entrepreneur or want to know what's involved in starting and running a nursery, our guides have got it covered and are also available as podcasts.

The UK's top entrepreneurs frequently talk to Startups.co.uk and you'll be able to read, listen and watch videos of the likes of Peter Jones, Anita Roddick, Stelios Haji Ioannou and Richard Branson telling their inspirational stories.

With an interactive forum and the opportunity to write your own blogs, Startups.co.uk also offers you the unique chance to network with other new business owners and raise your profile on a platform that attracts more than 150,000 visitors each month.

www.startups.co.uk

'Although in business there is no substitute for making the leap and getting started, there is much to be learned from entrepreneurs who have been there and done it. Live the highs and lows for yourself, but read this book first.'

Lord Bilimoria, founder & Chief Executive of Cobra